# 공략! OPIc IM3+

CARROT HOUSE

**OPIc 공략! IM3+**
© Carrot House

All rights reserved. No part of this publication may be reproduced,
stored in a retrieval system, or transmitted in any form or by any means
without the prior permission in writing of Carrot House

First published May 2017
Reprinted March 2018

**Author:** Carrot Language Research & Development, Canada

**ISBN** 978-89-6732-249-6

**Printed and distributed in Korea**
9F, 488 Gangnam St., Gangnam-gu, Seoul 06210, Korea

# Curriculum Map

| Course | Level 1 | Level 2 | Level 3 | Level 4 | Level 5 | Level 6 | Level 7 | Text Book |
|---|---|---|---|---|---|---|---|---|
| **General Conversation** | Essential English : Begin Again / Pre Get Up to Speed 1~2 | New Get Up to Speed 1 | New Get Up to Speed 2 | New Get Up to Speed 3 | New Get Up to Speed 4 | | | |
| | Daily Focused English 1 | Daily Focused English 2 | | | | | | |
| **Discussion** | | | | Active Discussion 1 | Active Discussion 2 | Dynamic Discussion | | |
| | | | | Chicken Soup Course | | | | |
| **Business Conversation** | Pre Business Basics 1 | Pre Business Basics 2 | Business Basics 1 | Business Basics 2 | Business Practice 1 | Business Practice 2 | | |
| **Global Biz Workshop** | | | | Effective Business Writing Skills (Workbook) | | | | |
| | | | | Effective Presentation Skills (Workbook) | | | | |
| | | | | | Effective Negotiation Skills (Workbook) | | | |
| | | | | | Cross-Cultural Training 1~2 (Workbook) | | | |
| | | | | | Leadership Training Course (Workbook) | | | |
| **Business Skills** | | | | Simple & Clear Technical Writing Skills | | | | |
| | | | | Effective Business Writing Skills | | | | |
| | | | | Effective Meeting Skills | | | | |
| | | | | Effective Presentation Skills | | | | |
| | | | | | Marketing 1 - 2 | | | |
| **On the Job English** | | | | Human Resources | | | | |
| | | | | Accounting and Finance | | | | |
| | | | | Marketing and Sales | | | | |
| | | | | Production Management | | | | |
| | | | | Automotive | | | | |
| | | | | Banking and Commerce | | | | |
| | | | | Medical and Medicine | | | | |
| | | | | Information Technology | | | | |
| | | | Construction English in Use 1 ~ 4 | | | | | |
| | | | Public Service English in Use | | | | | |
| **TEST Preparation** | | OPIc 도전! IM+ | | | ★OPIc 공략! IM3+ | | | |
| | | | | ATEC OPIc | | | | |
| | | | | How to Say it, Logically? | | | | |
| | | | TOEIC Speaking 도전! Level 5 | | | | | |
| | | | | TOEIC Speaking 공략! Level 7 | | | | |

※ This Curriculum Map illustrates the entire line-up of textbooks at CARROT HOUSE.

CARROT HOUSE _ 2017.05

# Introduction

## Carrot House Methodology

**Andragogical Approach & Productive English**

The teaching of children (pedagogy) and the teaching of adults (andragogy) are distinctively different. Pedagogy is akin to training and encourages convergent thinking and rote learning. It is compulsory, centered on the teacher and the imparting of information with minimal control by the learner. Andragogy, by contrast, is about education as freedom. It encourages divergent thinking and active learning. It is voluntary, learner oriented and opens up vistas for continuous learning. Adults need to feel independent and in control of their learning. Therefore, Carrot House curriculum is based on andragogy and is designed to involve learners' participation and engagement by providing more task-based activities and opportunities to frequently interact in the classroom.

People want to achieve communicative competence when they learn other languages. English education in EFL environments has been rather focused on receptive skills of English—listening and reading—which just increases learners' knowledge about language, not the competence of using them. If people are well equipped with productive skills—speaking and writing—they will be competent in English communication. This is why Carrot House curriculum is designed to enhance learners' productive skills throughout the course. This andragogical approach of the Carrot House Curriculum, which focuses on productive English, will enable learners to achieve communication skills necessary for global competence. Carrot House's teaching philosophy and curriculum combined pursues a "Language for Success" for all learners.

**Communicative Language Learning (CLL)**

This communicative interaction, the essential component of language acquisition, does not occur in a typical, non-meaningful, fun-oriented conversation with native speakers. It occurs in a negotiated interaction through which a well-trained teacher provides comprehensible input that is appropriate to the learners. The learners actively utilize the opportunities given to them by the teachers.

To this end, the Communicative Language Learning (CLL) method is employed in the field of Foreign Language Acquisition. CLL provides the activities that are geared toward using language pragmatically, authentically and functionally with the intention of achieving meaningful purposes.

# 목 차

OPIc 공략! IM3+

## I. OPIc 이해하기
- OPIc 이란? ..... 10
- Background Survey ..... 14
- OPIc FAQ ..... 16

## II. 실력 다지기

### Part 1 공통질문
- Unit 1. 자기소개 ..... 21
- Unit 2. 인물 묘사 ..... 29
- Unit 3. 장소 묘사 ..... 37
- Unit 4. 경험 말하기 ..... 45
- Unit 5. 비교하기 ..... 53
- Unit 6. 이슈(Issue) 묻기 ..... 61

### Part 2 설문주제

#### Category 1 여가활동
- Unit 7. 영화/TV 보기 ..... 71
- Unit 8. 쇼핑하기 ..... 79
- Unit 9. 공연/콘서트 보기 ..... 87
- Unit 10. 공원/캠핑 가기 ..... 95

#### Category 2 취미와 관심사
- Unit 11. 음악 감상하기 ..... 103
- Unit 12. 요리하기 ..... 111

#### Category 3 운동
- Unit 13. 조깅/걷기 ..... 119
- Unit 14. 하이킹/트레킹 ..... 127

#### Category 4 휴가와 출장
- Unit 15. 국내/해외 여행 ..... 135
- Unit 16. 집에서 휴가 보내기 ..... 143

### Part 3 롤플레이
- Unit 17. EVA에게 질문하기 ..... 153
- Unit 18. 전화해서 질문하기 ..... 161
- Unit 19. 대안 제시하기 ..... 169
- Unit 20. 상황 설명하기 ..... 177

### Part 4 돌발주제
- Unit 21. 재활용 ..... 187
- Unit 22. 지형 ..... 195
- Unit 23. 은행 ..... 203
- Unit 24. 호텔 ..... 211
- Unit 25. 교통 ..... 219
- Unit 26. 기술 ..... 227
- Unit 27. 지역행사 ..... 235

## III. 실전 OPIc
- Actual Test 1 ..... 244
- Actual Test 2 ..... 246

## IV. 부록
- IM-IH 학습가이드
- OPIc 가이드 라인
- OPIc 금지답변

# 교재구성 알아보기

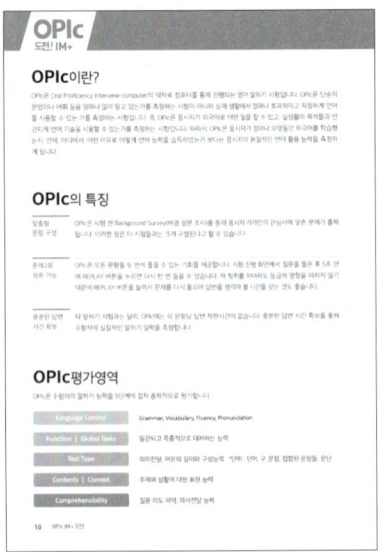

## 01 OPIc 이해하기
오픽 시험의 구성과 특징 및 평가영역에 대해 알아봅니다.

## 02 실력 다지기

### ○ Learning Objective
각 Unit의 학습목표가 제시됩니다.

### ○ Frequently Asked Questions
자주 출제되고 있는 질문을 미리 살펴봄으로써 주제별 질문유형을 이해하고 해당 학습내용을 파악합니다.

### ○ Brainstorming
학습자 수준에 따라 Brainstorming은 다음과 같이 진행됩니다.

 주제별 필수 어휘 및 표현을 브레인스토밍 합니다.

Step 2  브레인스토밍한 어휘 및 표현을 활용해 예상 질문을 만들어 봅니다.

## Key information
답변을 할 때 유용하게 사용할 수 있는 핵심 표현을 살펴봅니다.

- 샘플 문장을 통해 자신의 문장을 작성해 봅니다.
- 항목별로 작성된 문장을 배열하면 주제별 답변이 구성됩니다.

## How To Answer
출제가능성이 높은 질문에 대하여 답변 전략을 살펴봅니다.

## 1. 내용구성하기
답변구성에 필요한 내용을 살펴볼 수 있습니다.

## 2. Sample Answer
Answer tip!을 참고하여 보다 효과적인 답변 구성 전략을 파악합니다.

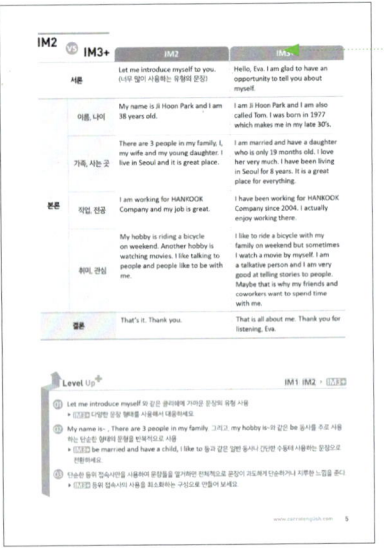

## IM2 vs IM3+

IM2 답변과 IM3+ 답변 비교 분석을 통해 고급 레벨을 달성하기 위한 전략을 알아 볼 수 있습니다.

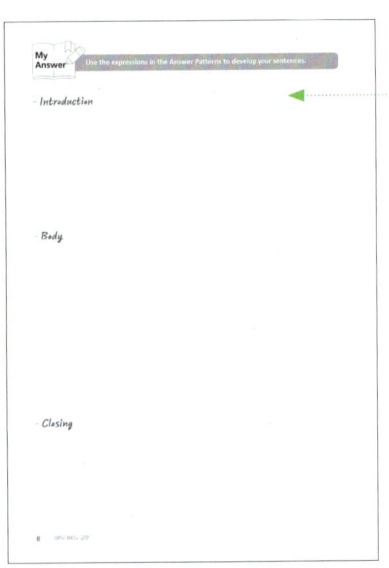

## My Answer

Answer patterns를 활용해 본인의 답변을 구성할 수 있습니다.

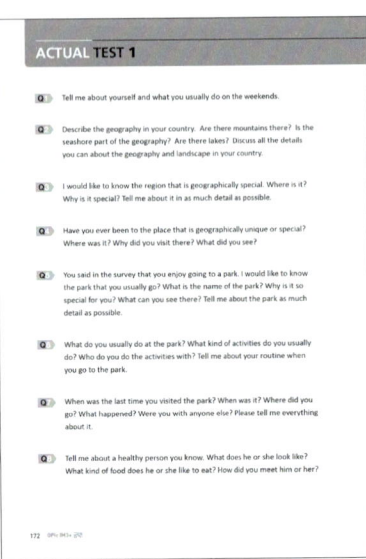

## 03 실전 OPIc

Actual Test 를 통해 실전감각을 키워 시험 준비를 마무리합니다.

* Actual Test는 MP3파일을 다운로드 받아 활용하시기 바랍니다.

# I

# OPIc 이해하기

- ☑ OPIc 이란?
- ☑ Background Survey
- ☑ OPIc FAQ

## OPIc이란?

OPIc은 Oral Proficiency Interview-computer의 약자로 컴퓨터를 통해 진행되는 영어 말하기 시험입니다. OPIc은 단순히 문법이나 어휘 등을 얼마나 많이 알고 있는가를 측정하는 시험이 아니라 실제 생활에서 얼마나 효과적이고 적절하게 언어를 사용할 수 있는 가를 측정하는 시험입니다. 즉, OPIc은 응시자가 외국어로 어떤 일을 할 수 있고, 실생활의 목적들과 연관되게 언어 기술을 사용할 수 있는가를 측정하는 시험입니다. 따라서, OPIc은 응시자가 얼마나 오랫동안 외국어를 학습했는지, 언제, 어디에서, 어떤 이유로 어떻게 언어 능력을 습득하였는가 보다는 응시자의 본질적인 언어 활용 능력을 측정하게 됩니다.

## OPIc의 특징

**맞춤형 문항 구성**
OPIc은 시험 전 Background Survey(배경 설문 조사)를 통해 응시자 개개인의 관심사에 맞춘 문제가 출제됩니다. 이러한 점은 타 시험들과는 크게 구별된다고 할 수 있습니다.

**문제2회 청취 가능**
OPIc은 모든 문항을 두 번씩 들을 수 있는 기회를 제공합니다. 시험 진행 화면에서 질문을 들은 후 5초 안에 REPLAY 버튼을 누르면 다시 한 번 들을 수 있습니다. 재 청취를 하더라도 등급에 영향을 미치지 않기 때문에 REPLAY 버튼을 눌러서 문제를 다시 들으며 답변을 생각해 볼 시간을 갖는 것도 좋습니다.

**충분한 답변 시간 확보**
타 말하기 시험과는 달리, OPIc에는 각 문항당 답변 제한시간이 없습니다. 충분한 답변 시간 확보를 통해 수험자의 실질적인 말하기 실력을 측정합니다.

## OPIc평가영역

OPIc은 수험자의 말하기 능력을 5단계에 걸쳐 총체적으로 평가합니다.

| | |
|---|---|
| **Language Control** | Grammar, Vocabulary, Fluency, Pronunciation |
| **Function | Global Tasks** | 일관되고 즉흥적으로 대처하는 능력 |
| **Text Type** | 의미전달, 어문의 길이와 구성능력  *단위 : 단어, 구, 문장, 접합된 문장들, 문단 |
| **Contents | Context** | 주제와 상황에 대한 표현 능력 |
| **Comprehensibility** | 질문 의도 파악, 의사전달 능력 |

# OPIc시험 진행 및 유형

## 시험진행구성

| 오리엔테이션 (약 20분) | ① Background Survey<br>② Self Assessment<br>③ Overview of OPIc<br>④ Sample Question | 시험 문항 출제를 위한 사전 설문<br>시험 난이도 결정을 위한 자가 평가<br>화면 구성, 문항 청취 및 답변 방법 안내<br>실제 답변 방법 연습 |
|---|---|---|
| 본 시험 (약 40분) | ① 1st Session<br>② 난이도 재조정<br>③ 2nd Session | 개인별 맞춤 문항 (질문 청취 2회 가능)<br>2차 Self Assessment (쉬운 질문, 비슷한 질문, 어려운 질문 중 택1)<br>1st와 동일 |
| 평가 및 통보 | ① 답변전송<br>② 평가<br>③ 결과 통보 | 인터넷을 통한 실시간 답변 전송<br>ACTFL 공인 Rater 신뢰도, 객관성 유지<br>근무일 기준 5일 내외의 신속한 평가 결과 통보 |

## 시험 문제 유형

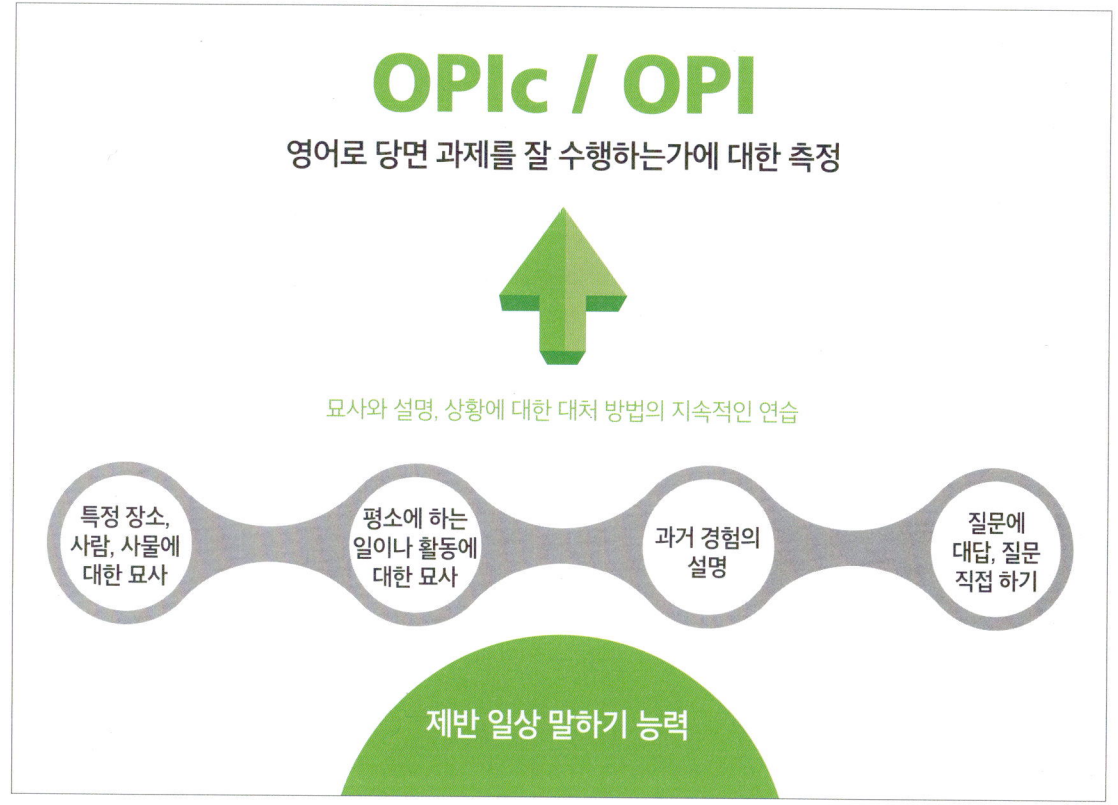

## 시험 응시화면

### Introduction
시험 전 응시 프로세스가 제시됩니다.

### 컴퓨터 설정
녹음 및 듣기 테스트를 통해 컴퓨터 환경을 설정합니다.

### Background Survey
시험 전 Background Survey를 통해 응시자 개개인의 관심사에 맞춘 문제가 출제됩니다.

### Self Assessment
6가지 등급의 설명을 읽고 각 등급의 샘플 답변을 들은 후 자기 실력에 맞는 등급(1~6등급)을 선택할 수 있습니다.

### 응시화면 가이드
응시화면 구성을 살펴봅니다. 시험 중 질문을 들은 후 5초안에 play 버튼을 클릭하면 질문을 재청취할 수 있습니다. 답변을 마친 후 Next 버튼을 클릭하면 다음 질문으로 넘어갑니다.

# OPIc등급 체계

OPIc의 모체인 OPI에서는 Advanced도 Low, Mid, High로 구분되지만, 컴퓨터로 시험을 보는 OPIc에서는 Advanced Low 라는 등급 하나만 부여됩니다.

| Level | 레벨별 요약설명 |
|---|---|
| AL (Advanced Low) | 다양한 사회적, 학술적 혹은 전문적 주제에 대한 요약문, 일상적인 서신을 능숙하게 작성할 수 있다. 적절한 시제를 활용함은 물론 복잡한 문장구조도 활용하여 다양한 문단 및 단락을 구성하며 글의 내용은 대부분의 원어민들이 쉽게 이해할 수 있다. |
| IH (Intermediate High) | 직장이나 학교에서 필요로 하는 과제에 대하여 다양한 글쓰기가 가능하다. 현재시제 외 기타시제도 활용하지만 약간의 오류를 범하기도 한다. 아이디어를 구성할 수 있고 친숙한 주제 혹은 사건에 관하여 묘사는 물론 요약 및 서술도 가능하다. 글의 내용은 대부분의 원어민들이 이해할 수 있다. |
| IM (Intermediate Mid) | 직장이나 학교에서 필요로 하는 기본적인 글쓰기가 가능하다. 간단한 요약문을 작성 할 수 있고 일상적인 업무와 관련된 서신을 주고 받을 수 있다. 다양한 문장으로 구성된 문단을 작성할 수 있으며, 현재시제 외 기타시제도 가끔 정확하게 활용할 수 있다. 글의 주요 내용은 대부분의 원어민들이 이해할 수 있다. |
| IL (Intermediate Low) | 친숙한 소재에 관하여 간단한 의견이나 질문 내용을 작성할 수 있다. 주로 현재시제를 활용하지만, 주어-동사-목적어 구조로 활용하여 간단한 의견교환은 할 수 있다. |
| NH (Novice High) | 간단한 단어나 어구를 활용하여 기본적인 작문을 할 수 있다. 어휘 및 문법에 대한 이해 부족으로 인하여 작성한 글이 원어민에 의해 부분적으로만 이해할 수 있다. 친숙한 소재에 관하여 짧은 메시지, 엽서, 리스트 등을 작성할 수 있다. |
| NM (Novice Mid) | 이미 암기한 친숙한 단어나 구를 활용할 수 있다. |
| NL (Novice Low) | 매우 제한적으로 몇몇 단어 및 구를 나열할 수 있다. |

# BACKGROUND SURVEY

이 Background Survey 응답을 기초로 개인 맞춤형 문항이 출제 됩니다.
질문을 자세히 읽고 답변해 주시기 바랍니다.

### 1. 현재 귀하는 어느 분야에 종사하고 계십니까?

☐ 사업/회사
☐ 자택근무/재택사업
☐ 교사/교육자
☐ 군복무
☐ 일 경험 없음

### 2. 현재 귀하는 학생이십니까?

☐ 네
☐ 아니오

### 3. 현재 귀하는 어디에 살고 계십니까?

☐ 개인 주택이나 아파트에 거주
☐ 친구나 룸메이트와 함께 주택이나 아파트에서 거주
☐ 가족(배우자/자녀/기타 가족 일원)과 함께 주택이나 아파트에 거주
☐ 학교 기숙사
☐ 군대 막사

아래의 4~7번 문항에서 12개 이상을 선택해 주시기 바랍니다.

### 4. 귀하의 여가 활동으로 주로 무엇을 하십니까? (두 개 이상 선택)

☐ 쇼핑 하기
☐ TV 시청
☐ 리얼리티 쇼 시청
☐ 영화 보기
☐ 클럽/나이트클럽 가기
☐ 공연 보기
☐ 콘서트 보기
☐ 박물관 가기
☐ 공원 가기
☐ 캠핑하기

☐ 해변 가기
☐ 스포츠 관람
☐ 주거 개선(=집안일 거들기)
☐ 술집/바에 가기
☐ 카페/커피 전문점에 가기
☐ 게임 하기
　(비디오, 카드, 보드, 휴대폰 등)
☐ 당구치기
☐ 체스 하기
☐ SNS에 글 올리기

☐ 친구들과 문자 대화하기
☐ 시험대비 과정 수강하기
☐ 뉴스를 보거나 듣기
☐ 요리 관련 프로그램 시청하기
☐ 차로 드라이브하기
☐ 스파/마사지샵 가기
☐ 구직 활동하기
☐ 자원 봉사하기

## 5. 귀하의 취미나 관심사는 무엇입니까? (한 개 이상 선택)

- ☐ 독서
- ☐ 아이에게 책 읽어 주기
- ☐ 음악 감상하기
- ☐ 악기 연주하기
- ☐ 혼자 노래 부르거나 합창하기
- ☐ 춤추기
- ☐ 글쓰기(편지, 단편, 시 등)
- ☐ 그림 그리기
- ☐ 요리하기
- ☐ 애완동물 기르기
- ☐ 주식 투자하기
- ☐ 신문 읽기
- ☐ 여행 관련 잡지나 블로그 읽기
- ☐ 사진 촬영하기

## 6. 귀하는 주로 어떤 운동을 즐기십니까? (한 개 이상 선택)

- ☐ 농구
- ☐ 야구/소프트볼
- ☐ 축구
- ☐ 미식축구
- ☐ 하키
- ☐ 크리켓
- ☐ 골프
- ☐ 배구
- ☐ 테니스
- ☐ 배드민턴
- ☐ 탁구
- ☐ 수영
- ☐ 자전거
- ☐ 스키/스노보드
- ☐ 아이스 스케이트
- ☐ 조깅
- ☐ 걷기
- ☐ 요가
- ☐ 하이킹/트레킹
- ☐ 낚시
- ☐ 태권도
- ☐ 운동 수영 수강하기
- ☐ 운동을 전혀 하지 않음

## 7. 귀하는 어떤 휴가나 출장을 다녀온 경험이 있습니까? (한 개 이상 선택)

- ☐ 국내 출장
- ☐ 해외 출장
- ☐ 집에서 보내는 휴가
- ☐ 국내 여행
- ☐ 해외 여행

# OPIc FAQ

**01** **시험 당일 무엇을 준비해야 하나요?**

시험 당일에는 규정 신분증(주민등록증, 운전면허증, 기간 만료 전 여권, 공무원증 등)을 반드시 지참해야 합니다. 말하기 시험이기 때문에 필기도구 등은 필요하지 않으며 시험이 진행되는 동안에는 컴퓨터 및 게시판을 통해 시간확인을 할 수 있습니다.

**02** **시험응시 도중 필기도구를 사용하여 답변을 준비해도 되나요?**

OPIc 응시자는 필기도구를 가지고 시험장에 입실할 수 없습니다. 따라서 시험 중에 필기도구를 이용하여 메모 등을 하실 수 없으며, 적발 시 부정행위로 처리되어 OPIc 시험 규정에 따라 향후 시험 응시 기회에 제한을 받습니다.

**03** **Self-Assessment란 무엇인가요?**

Self-Assessment는 난이도 선택을 일컫습니다. OPIc은 본시험 1차와 본시험 2차로 크게 나뉩니다. 본시험 1차는 시험 전에 선택했던 난이도의 수준에 맞는 문제가 출제되는 것이고, 본시험 2차는 본시험 1차를 치른 후 난이도 재조정에서 새롭게 선택한 난이도에 맞는 문제가 출제됩니다. 난이도 재조정에서는 '쉬운 질문, 비슷한 질문, 어려운 질문'중에서 선택하게 됩니다.

**04** **시험 보는 중간에 Self-Assessment로 레벨을 변경하는 것이 성적에 영향을 미치나요?**

처음에 높은 레벨로 시작했다가 중간에 낮은 레벨로 바꾸거나, 그 반대로 낮은 레벨에서 시작해서 높은 레벨로 바꾸는 자체로는 성적이 바뀌지 않습니다. 철저히 주어진 답변에 얼마나 충실하게 답변했는지가 성적을 좌우한다고 보면 됩니다. 그러나, 본인이 영어 실력과 너무 동떨어진 레벨을 선택하는 것은 바람직하지 않습니다.

**05** 난이도에 따라 문제수가 달라지나요?

OPIc은 Self-Assessment에서 선택한 난이도(총 1~6단계)에 따라 12~15개의 문제가 출제됩니다.

1~2단계에서는 보통 12문제가 출제되고 난이도 초급으로 분류할 수 있습니다. 이 단계에서는 보통 항목당 두 문제 정도가 출제되고 문제 빠르기와 난이도가 비슷하다고 할 수 있습니다.

3~4단계에서는 15문제가 출제되며 난이도 중급으로 이해할 수 있습니다. 3단계와 4단계의 난이도는 큰 차이가 없으므로 IL~IM등급을 준비하고 있다면 3~4단계를 선택하면 됩니다.
3단계 이상부터는 항목당 세 문제, 즉 Three Combo 문제가 등장하게 됩니다.

5~6단계 역시 15문제가 출제되며 난이도는 고급에 해당됩니다. 최고 난이도답게 3~4단계 수준의 문제 이외에 다소 어려운 시사 관련 문제가 등장합니다. 따라서 초·중·고급 난이도의 차이점을 정확하게 이해하고 선택하는 것이 중요합니다.

**06** Background Survey 내용과 관련이 없는 문제도 출제되나요?

OPIc은 Background Survey를 통해 수험자의 개인 맞춤형 문항출제가 가능하지만 다른 영역의 질문 또한 출제되어 수험자가 예상하지 못한 문제에 대한 상황 대처능력 및 순발력 또한 평가합니다. 따라서, Background Survey에서 선택한 내용과 다른 문제가 출제되더라도 최선을 다해 성실하게 답변하는 것이 좋습니다.

**07** 문제를 반복해서 들으면 성적에 안 좋은 영향을 미치나요?

문제를 반복 청취하는 것이 성적에 직접적으로 영향을 미치는 것은 아닙니다. 하지만 문제를 반복 청취했을 때 답변 시간이 줄어들 수밖에 없으므로, 시간 관리에 어려움을 느낄 수도 있습니다. OPIc 문제의 답변 시간은 질문 청취 시간을 제외하고 약 35분 가량입니다. 따라서 주어진 시간 내 모든 문제에 효율적으로 답변할 수 있도록 시간을 활용해야 합니다.

**08** 성적이 UR이라고 나오는 것은 무엇을 의미하나요?

"UR"은 unable to rate을 의미합니다. UR은 녹음 불량, 녹음 음량이 너무 작은 경우, 수험자가 답변을 하지 않은 경우에 해당합니다. 수험자의 과실인 경우 응시료 환불 및 재시험의 기회가 주어지지 않습니다. 반면, 시스템적인 오류로 UR이 나왔을 경우 한 번의 재시험 기회를 드립니다.

# OPIc 공략! IM3+

# 실력다지기

## ☑ Part 1 공통질문

Unit 1 | 자기소개
Unit 2 | 인물 묘사
Unit 3 | 장소 묘사
Unit 4 | 경험 말하기
Unit 5 | 비교하기
Unit 6 | 이슈(Issue) 묻기

*I've missed more than 9000 shots in my career.*
*I've lost almost 300 games. 26 times I've been trusted to take the game winning shot and missed.*
*I've failed over and over and over again in my life. And that is why I succeed.*

Michael Jordan
(1963~Present) American former professional basketball player

# OPIc
## 공략! IM3+

**UNIT 1**

## 자기소개

# UNIT 01 자기소개

OPIc 공략! IM3+

## Learning Objectives
성격 및 외모에 관한 다양한 형용사들을 활용하여 자신을 소개할 수 있다.

## Frequently Asked Questions

**기본형**
- Please briefly tell me about yourself and your family.
- Tell me a little bit about yourself and what you do for living.

**취미와 흥미 결합형**
- Tell me about yourself, your job, what you do in your free time, and your hobbies.
- Tell me about yourself and what your interests are.

## Brainstorming

**Step 1** Brainstorm key words and expressions about the topic.
**Step 2** Use the words and expressions to brainstorm possible questions.

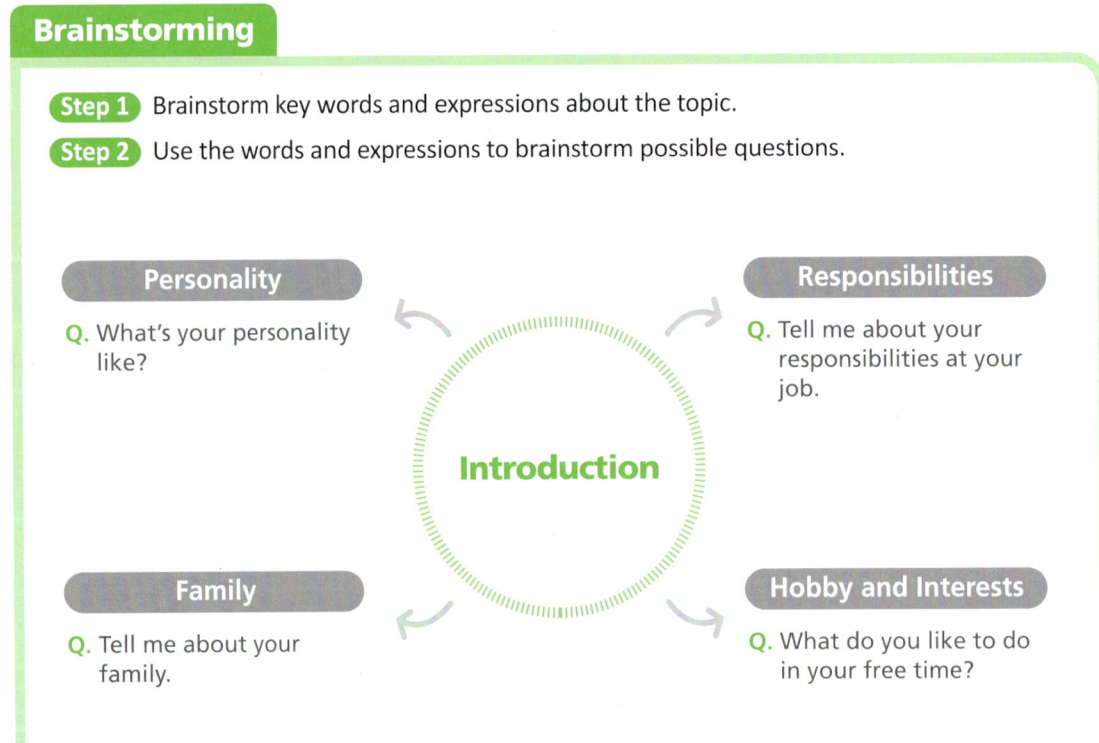

**Personality**
Q. What's your personality like?

**Responsibilities**
Q. Tell me about your responsibilities at your job.

**Family**
Q. Tell me about your family.

**Hobby and Interests**
Q. What do you like to do in your free time?

Introduction

## Key Information

### 이름, 나이

I am 이름 but you can call me 별명/영어이름 I am in my 나이대.
제 이름은 이름입니다만, 별명/영어이름라고 불러주세요. 전 나이대 입니다.

▶ In my early 20's 20대 초반
  Mid 30's 30대 중반
  Late 40's 40대 후반

### 가족과 사는 곳

I am married and have         children(daughter/son/child).
전 결혼했고    명의 자녀(딸, 아들, 아이들)가 있습니다.

I am not married and live alone/with 같이 사는 가족.
전 미혼이고 혼자/같이 사는 가족 와 살고 있습니다.

I have been living in 장소 for 기간.
전 기간 동안 장소에서 살고 있는 중입니다.

▶ 결혼은 상태를 나타내므로 현재 결혼한 상태라면 항상 현재형을 써야함.
  I was married 는 나는 결혼을 했지만 현재는 결혼한 상태가 아니다 라는 의미

### 전공이나 직업

I have been working for/at 직장 for 기간/ since 일을 시작한 년도.
기간동안/일을 시작한 년도부터 직장에서 근무하고 있습니다.

I am in charge of 관련 일.
관련 일을 맡고 있습니다.

I am a university(college) student at 대학교 이름. I major in 전공.
대학교명/전문대/대학교를 다니고 있습니다. 제 전공은 전공입니다.

### 취미와 관심

I like/love to 취미 활동 with 사람 in my free time.
저는 여가시간에 사람과 취미활동하는 걸 좋아합니다.

▶ My hobby is라는 단순한 형태의 문장 형식 탈피.
  I like/love 다음에는 to농사 원형의 to부정사 혹은 동사원형-ing 형태의 동명사 둘다 사용 가능

### 성격

I am a 성격 person.
저는 성격한 사람입니다.

I am good at 장점.
저는 장점을 잘 합니다.

---

**Answer tips!**

첫인상을 결정하는 질문인 만큼 자기소개를 충분히 연습해두는 것이 중요합니다. 자기소개를 가장 자연스럽게 풀어가는 방법은 이름과 나이, 하는 일, 가족관계, 성격, 취미 및 여가활동 등에 관하여 이야기하면 됩니다. 성격 및 외모에 관한 형용사들을 충분히 활용하여 답변내용을 풍부히 구성하는 것이 중요합니다. Eva에게 말하는 것 같은 친근한 표현을 대답 앞뒤에 사용하는 것도 좋습니다.

## How to Answer

**Q1.** I would like you to tell me about yourself briefly.

| 내용구성하기 | Introduction | ☑ 이름과 나이 | | | |
|---|---|---|---|---|---|
| | Body | ☑ 가족관계 | ☑ 직업 | ☑ 취미 | ☑ 성격 |
| | Closing | ☑ 느낌 및 의견 | | | |

### Introduction

Hello, Eva. I am glad to have an opportunity to tell you about myself.

### Body

I am Ji Hoon Park but you can call me Tom. I was born in 1977, which puts me ❶ **in my late 30's.**

I am married and have a daughter who is only 19 months old. I love her very much. I ❷ **have been living** in Seoul for 8 years. It is a great place for everything.

I have been working for HANKOOK since 2004. I enjoy working there very much.

I like to cycle with my family on the weekend but sometimes I watch movies by myself. I am a talkative person and I enjoy telling stories to people. Maybe ❸ **that is why my friends** and co-workers want to spend time with me.

### Closing

I enjoyed telling you about myself. Thank you for listening, Eva.

### Useful Expressions

❶ Be in one's early/mid/late 20/30/40's
   20대/30대/40대 초/중반/후반입니다.
   ▶ I am in my late 30's.

❷ Have been+V (present progressive) in (location) for (time duration)
   ▶ I have been living in Seoul for 8 years.

❸ That is why+S-V
   그것이 왜 주어 동사하는 이유이다.
   ▶ Maybe that is why people want to spend time with me.

# IM2  IM3+

| | | IM2 | IM3+ |
|---|---|---|---|
| **Introduction** | | Let me introduce myself to you. | Hello, Eva. I am glad to have an opportunity to tell you about myself. |
| **Body** | 이름과 나이 | My name is Ji Hoon Park and I am 38 years old. | I am Ji Hoon Park but you can call me Tom. I was born in 1977, which puts me in my late 30s. |
| | 가족관계 및 사는 곳 | There are 3 people in my family: my wife, my young daughter, and me. I live in Seoul and it is great place. | I am married and have a daughter who is only 19 months old. I love her very much. I have been living in Seoul for 8 years. It is a great place for everything. |
| | 직업 | I work for HANKOOK and my job is great. | I have been working for HANKOOK since 2004. I enjoy working there very much. |
| | 취미 및 성격 | My hobby is cycling on the weekend. Another hobby of mine is watching movies. I like talking to people and people like to be with me. | I like to cycle with my family on the weekend but sometimes I watch movies by myself. I am a talkative person and I enjoy telling stories to people. Maybe that is why my friends and co-workers want to spend time with me. |
| **Closing** | | That's it. Thank you. | I enjoyed telling you about myself. Thank you for listening, Eva. |

**01** Let me introduce myself 와 같은 클리쉐에 가까운 문장의 유형 사용
▶ **IM3+** 다양한 문장 형태를 사용해서 대응하세요.

**02** My name is... , There are 3 people in my family, 그리고, My hobby is...와 같은 be 동사를 주로 사용하는 단순한 형태의 문형을 반복적으로 사용
▶ **IM3+** be married and have a child, I like to 등과 같은 일반 동사나 간단한 수동태 사용하는 문장으로 전환하세요.

**03** 단순한 등위 접속사만을 사용하여 문장들을 열거하면 전체적으로 문장이 과도하게 단순하거나 지루한 느낌을 준다.
▶ **IM3+** 등위 접속사의 사용을 최소화하는 구성으로 만들어 보세요.

**Q2.** Tell me about yourself and what you usually do on the weekends.

**내용구성하기**
- **Introduction** ☑ 이름과 나이
- **Body** ☑ 전공  ☑ 현재 하는 일  ☑ 가족관계
- **Closing** ☑ 느낌 및 의견

### Introduction

How do you do, Eva? Nice to meet you.

### Body

I am a student majoring in economics at Hankook University. Now that I am ❶ **in my senior year**, I am ❷ **trying to** look for a job. I want a job where I can experience various things and meet a lot of new people.

I have been living with my sister for 3 years. She and I are best friends. We like to watch movies and go to concerts together when we have free time. Since I ❸ **am busy studying** and preparing for job interviews now, I do not have much time to ❹ **hang out with** my sister. But she understands what I am going through and tries to support me.

I am an easy going person who likes to think of the future optimistically. I am also good at listening to others. Maybe that is why my friends like me.

### Closing

That is all. Thank you.

**Useful Expressions**

❶ In one's senior year
대학 4학년의
▶ She is in her senior year.

❷ Trying to...
~하려고 한다
▶ Trying to...

❸ Busy -ing
~하느라 바쁘다.
▶ I am busy studying.

❹ Hang out with...
~와 어울리다.
▶ I like to hang out with my sister.

## Q3. Tell me a little bit about yourself and what you do for living.

**내용구성하기**
- **Introduction** ☑ 인사하기
- **Body** ☑ 이름과 나이  ☑ 전공과 현재 하는 일  ☑ 가족관계 및 여가활동  ☑ 성격
- **Closing** ☑ 느낌 및 의견

### Introduction
Alright. I am very excited to tell you about myself. My name is Hyun and I am 34 years old.

### Body
I **❶ graduated from** college about 6 years ago and I am currently working for ABC Company. I actually started to work at this company a year ago. Before that, I traveled around the world and enjoyed different experiences.

During that part of my life, I **❷ encountered** many interesting and strange situations and learned a lot from them. **❸ The primary reason** that ABC Company hired me was that they were looking for a person who is not afraid of dealing with the unexpected.

### Closing
This is the end of my story. Hope you enjoyed my introduction, Eva.

### Useful Expressions

❶ Graduate from...
~를 졸업하다.
▶ I graduated from college 6 years ago.

❷ Encounter
맞닥뜨리다.
▶ I encountered many interesting situations.

❸ The primary reason
주된 이유.
▶ The primary reason the company hired me is because of my personality.

**My Answer** — Use the expressions from the Key Information to develop your sentences.

– Introduction

– Body

– Closing

# OPIc
## 공략! IM3+

**UNIT 2**

## 인물 묘사

# UNIT 02 인물 묘사

OPIc 공략! IM3+

## Learning Objectives

본인주위의 인물이나 특정 직업의 인물을 묘사할 수 있다.

## Frequently Asked Questions

- Tell me about your friend. How did you meet him first? What does he look like?
- Describe one of your neighbors. How was her first impression? What does she look like?
- Do you know anyone who is healthy? What is his/her name? Why do you think he/she is healthy?
- I would like to know about an actor or actress you like the most.
- Can you describe to me a musician you like the most?

## Brainstorming

Step 1  Brainstorm key words and expressions about the topic.
Step 2  Use the words and expressions to brainstorm possible questions.

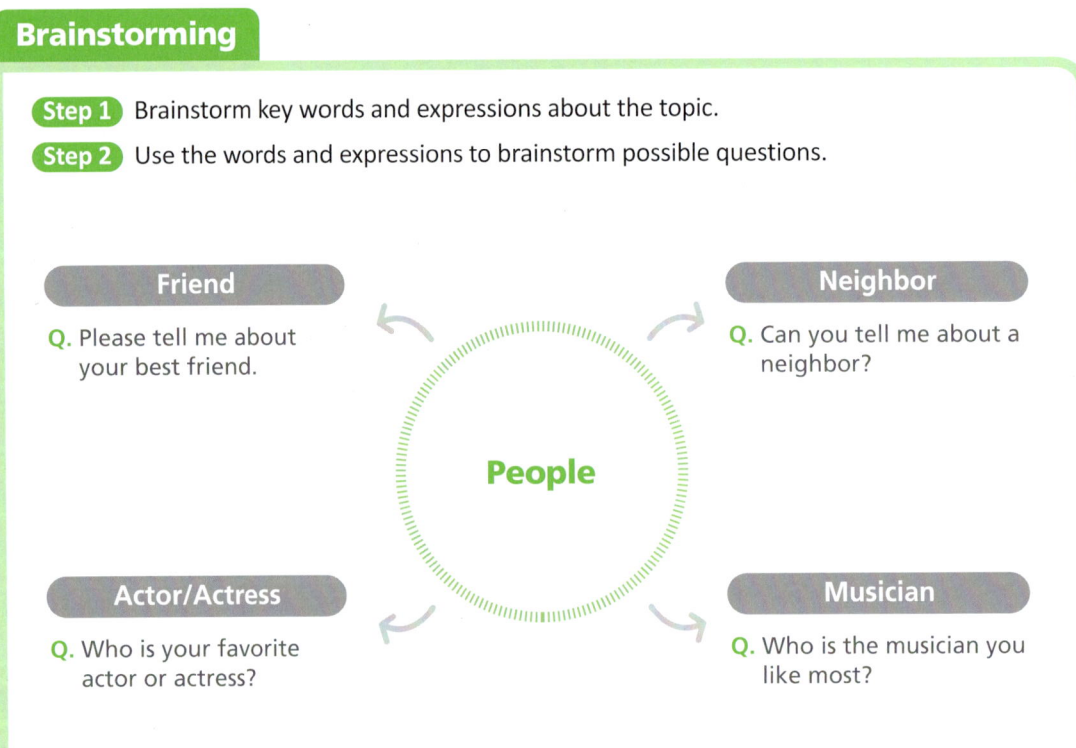

**Friend**
Q. Please tell me about your best friend.

**Neighbor**
Q. Can you tell me about a neighbor?

**People**

**Actor/Actress**
Q. Who is your favorite actor or actress?

**Musician**
Q. Who is the musician you like most?

# Key Information

### 이름과 기본정보

The 사람 whom I would like to talk about is 사람 이름.
내가 얘기하고 싶은 사람은 사람이름입니다.

▶ Want 보다 좀 더 공손하고 형식적인 would like 사용. Want와 마찬가지로 to부정사를 목적어로 사용한다

### 처음 알게 된 경위(첫인상)

I have known 사람 for 기간/ since 처음 알게 된 시기.
저는 사람을 처음 알게 된 시기부터 기간동안 알고 지냈습니다.

I saw him/her in/at 장소 first.
그/그녀를 장소에서 만났습니다.

My first impression of him/her was _____.
그/그녀의 첫인상은 _____ 했습니다.

Since then, he/she has been my _____.
그때 이후 그/그녀는 나의 _____ 이 됐습니다.

▶ 현재 완료 문형에서 for와 since
For 다음에는 기간/셀 수 있는 명사
Since 다음에는 시작된 시점. 과거를 나타내는 부사 사용 가능

### 외모

He/She is good-looking/handsome/pretty/beautiful/plain/cute with light/dark skin.
그/그녀는 잘생긴/핸섬한/예쁜/아름다운/평범한/귀여운 외모로, 흰/까무잡잡한 피부입니다.

He/She has long/short straight/curly black/brown/dark brown hair.
그/그녀는 긴/짧은 생/곱슬 검은색/갈색/짙은 갈색 머리입니다.

Sometimes, people say he/she resembles/ looks like 닮은 사람.
가끔 사람들은 그/그녀가 닮은 사람을 닮았다고 합니다.

### 좋아하는 이유

He/She is a warm-hearted/outgoing/hardworking/kind/warm/humorous/funny/brilliant person.
그/그녀는 마음씨가 따뜻한/활달한/성실한/친절한/온화한/유머러스/재미있는/똑똑한 사람입니다.

인물 묘사의 문제이지만 답변을 인물 묘사에만 집중할 필요는 없습니다. 자칫 문장의 구조가 단조롭고 지루해 질 수 있습니다. 오히려 처음 만나게 된 경위나 첫인상에 관련된 에피소드와 적절하게 분배하여 사용합니다. 부정적인 묘사를 하는 것은 피하는 것이 좋습니다.

## How to Answer

**Q1.** Tell me about one of your neighbors. What is his or her name? How did you become close? What does he or she look like? Why do you like to hang out with him or her? Describe your neighbor in as much detail as possible.

| 내용구성하기 | Introduction | ☑ 이름 | | | |
|---|---|---|---|---|---|
| | Body | ☑ 첫인상 | ☑ 처음 알게된 경위 | ☑ 외모 | ☑ 성격 알고지낸 기간 |
| | Closing | ☑ 느낌 및 의견 | | | |

### Introduction
I am glad you asked. The neighbor whom I would like to talk about is Mrs. Kim.

### Body
She has been living next door to me for almost five years. I see her every day.

I ❶ **have actually known her well for about a year since last New Year's** Day. Last year, I was unable to go home for the holiday and she asked me to have dinner with her family. She ❷ **made me feel right at home.** ❸ **Since then**, she has become one of my closest friends.

She is in her early 40s but she looks much younger than her age. She is tall and has a slim figure. Sometimes, people say ❹ **she resembles** a famous Korean actress. I think she enjoys people saying that.

Even though there is an age gap of almost 10 years between us, we have similar personalities. I like her because I am able to relate to her well. Her family also loves her since she is a warm-hearted person.

### Closing
I hope we can stay neighbors and great friends for a long time.

---

**Useful Expressions**

❶ Have known (person) for (time period)
(기간) 동안 (사람)을 알아왔다.
▸ I have known her for 5 years.

❷ Make one feel right at home
집처럼 느끼게 해주다.
▸ She made me feel right at home.

❸ Since then...
그 이후로
▸ We have studied English even harder since then.

❹ He/She resembles...
그/그녀는 (사람)을 닮다.
▸ She resembles a famous actress.

# IM2 vs IM3+

| | IM2 | IM3+ |
|---|---|---|
| **Introduction** | My neighbor's name is Mrs. Kim. | I am glad you asked. The neighbor whom I would like to talk about is Mrs. Kim. |
| **Body** — 기본 정보 | | She has been living next door to me for almost five years. I see her every day. |
| **Body** — 첫인상 | I got to know her well last year after she invited me to her home on New Year's Day. | I have actually known her well for about a year since last New Year's Day. Last year, I was unable to go home for the holiday and she asked me to have dinner with her family. She made me feel right at home. Since then, she has become one of my closest friends. |
| **Body** — 외모 | She is around 40. She is tall and slim, and she is pretty. | She is in her early 40s but she looks much younger than her age. She is tall and has a slim figure. Sometimes, people say she resembles a famous Korean actress. I think she enjoys people saying that. |
| **Body** — 성격 | She is 10 years older than me but I like her because she is warm and we have similar personalities. | Even though there is an age gap of almost 10 years between us, we have similar personalities. I like her because I am able to relate to her well. Her family also loves her since she is a warm-hearted person. |
| **Closing** | I hope we can stay neighbors for a long time. | I hope we can stay neighbors and great friends for a long time. |

## Level Up+

### IM1~IM2?

**01** My neighbor's name is... 와 같은 be 동사를 주로 사용하는 단순한 형태의 문형
▶ 다양한 문장 형태를 사용해서 대응하세요.

**02** I started to know her last year과 같은 현재 완료를 사용할 수 있는 여지가 있는 문장을 단순한 과거형 문장으로 사용.
▶ 현재 완료 문형으로 전환하여 사용하세요.

**03** 외모 묘사를 단순한 표현으로 사용했고 등위접속사 and로 연결되어 있는 여러 개의 반복적인 단문으로 구성
▶ 외모 관련 다양한 표현을 시도하고 앞 문장의 형태와 뒷 문장의 형태를 다르게 구성하려고 노력하세요.

**Q2.** I would like you to tell me about one of your best friends. When did you meet him or her for the first time and how did you become best friends. Please describe your best friend in detail.

| 내용구성하기 | | |
|---|---|---|
| **Introduction** | ☑ 이름 | |
| **Body** | ☑ 첫만남과 친해지게 된 계기 | ☑ 좋아하는 이유 |
| **Closing** | ☑ 느낌 및 의견 | |

### Introduction

The friend whom I would like to speak about is my best friend Jane.

### Body

We went to the same college. I met her on the first day of college. We ❶ **were assigned to** the same class and were both nervous about everything. As an ❷ **icebreaking** game, a professor asked us to write down our favorite movie, musician, and hobby, and find one person that we had ❸ **something in common** with. Surprisingly, Jane and I wrote the exact same answers. We spent the first class talking about all the things we had in common. That is how we first became close.

Since we share so many similar interests, we have plenty of nice memories together in college. I really like her a lot. Also, she is great at listening to people and giving reasonable advice so people love spending time with her.

### Closing

It would be nice if everyone could have a friend as dear to them as Jane is to me.

### Useful Expressions

❶ Be assigned to...
~로 배정 되다.
▶ We were assigned to the same class.

❷ Icebreaking
안면 트기, 어색함을 풀기 위한 말하기
▶ We started with an icebreaking game.

❸ Something in common
무언가 공통점의
▶ It's hard to find someone with something in common with you.

**Q3.** Do you have a musician whose music you like to listen to the most? If you do, tell me who he or she is. What kind of music does he or she play? What does he or she look like? What is his or her most famous work? Describe the musician you like the most as much as possible.

| 내용구성하기 | Introduction | ☑ 음악가 이름 | | |
|---|---|---|---|---|
| | Body | ☑ 처음 알게 된 계기상 | ☑ 외모 묘사상 | ☑ 좋아하는 이유 |
| | Closing | ☑ 느낌 및 의견 | | |

### Introduction

Among my favorite musicians, I like Morrissey the best. He is a famous British singer.

### Body

I first listened to his music when my friend introduced me to one of his albums. At the time, I enjoyed it but did not think much about it until I heard one of his songs on the radio later. I ❶ **remember driving** along and thinking his song was a perfect fit for the drizzling rain outside the car window. That is how I got into him and his music.

He ❷ **used to be tall and skinny** but recently he has gained some weight. His hair is now gray and he sometimes wears glasses.

But his songs and lyrics do not feel old. He can still make beautiful music.

### Closing

If you have not had a chance to listen to his songs, I really urge you to take some time to listen to them. You won't regret it.

**Useful Expressions**

❶ Remember -ing
-ing 했던 것은 기억한다.
▶ remember singing along to the song.

❷ Used to +V
(동사)하곤 했다.
▶ He used to be short, but now he is tall.

 **My Answer** — Use the expressions from the Key Information to develop your sentences.

— Introduction

— Body

— Closing

# OPIc
## 공략! IM3+

### UNIT 3
## 장소 묘사

# UNIT 03 장소 묘사

OPIc 공략! IM3+

## Learning Objectives

장소의 위치, 역할 및 기능, 특징 등에 대해 묘사하거나, 특정 장소와 개인 혹은 조직의 관계, 그리고 장소에 대한 개인적인 생각과 의견에 대해 답할 수 있다.

## Frequently Asked Questions

- I would like you to describe the movie theater that you go to most often. What is it called? Where is it located? What does it look like? Describe it to me.
- Where is the park you usually go? What is the name of the park and what can we see there?
- Describe the house you live in. Where do you live? What does it look like?
- Can you tell me about the place you like the most or your room at your house?

## Brainstorming

**Step 1** Brainstorm key words and expressions about the topic.
**Step 2** Use the words and expressions to brainstorm possible questions.

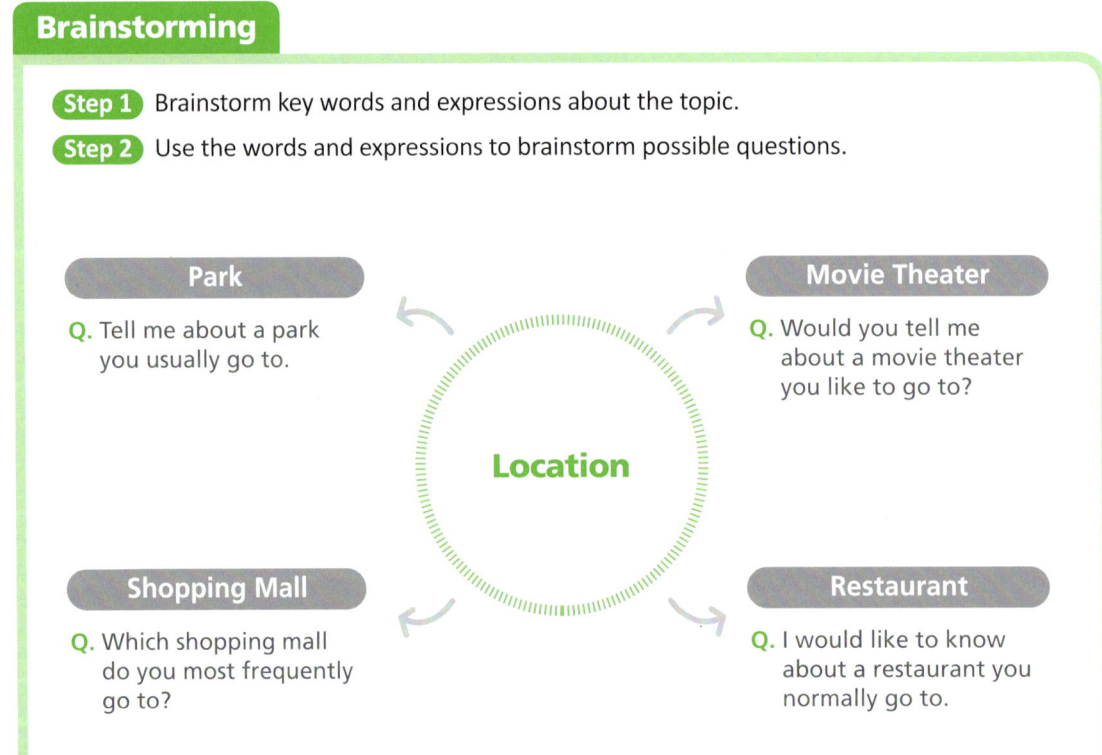

**Park**
Q. Tell me about a park you usually go to.

**Movie Theater**
Q. Would you tell me about a movie theater you like to go to?

**Location**

**Shopping Mall**
Q. Which shopping mall do you most frequently go to?

**Restaurant**
Q. I would like to know about a restaurant you normally go to.

## Key Information

### 이름과 장소

The place I like to go to is 이름. It is located in 장소.
내가 즐겨 가는 장소는 이름입니다. 그것은 장소에 위치해 있습니다.

▶ The place which/that I like to go 관계대명사가 사용된 문장으로 목적격 관계대명사는 생략되어 있다.

### 외부묘사

It is in a 숫자-story building.
그것은 숫자층짜리 건물에 있습니다.

You can find _____ near there.
그 근방에서 _____ 를 볼 수 있습니다.

_____ can be seen around it.
_____ 가 주변에 있습니다.

▶ 몇 층짜리 건물 할 때 에는 floor가 아닌 story를 사용한다. 예를 들어 7층짜리 건물 하면 7-story building 으로 표현하면 적절하다.

### 내부묘사

On the 서수 floor
기수 층에

_____ is located/situated/placed _____.
_____ 는 _____ 에 위치해/자리잡고/장소에 있습니다.

You can see _____.
_____ 가 보입니다.

▶ ~있다라는 묘사를 할 때 there is/are 문형만을 사용하면 답변이 지루해 질 수 있으니 be located/situated/placed 나 you can see/find와 같은 여러가지 문형을 사용하는 것이 좋다.

### 이유

Big parking lots
대형 주차장

Easy access by public transportation
대중교통 접근성 편리

New and clean
새롭고 깨끗함

Refreshing atmosphere
상쾌한 분위기

주제에 맞는 키워드를 3가지 생각하고 말하기를 시작하면 쉽습니다. 집을 묘사할 때 집안에서 보이는 것들만 묘사하기보다는 집 주변에 있는 시설이나 주위 환경을 함께 묘사하면 좋습니다.

## How to Answer

**Q1.** Please tell me about your favorite restaurant. Where is it located? How is it decorated? What do you like about the place? Please describe the restaurant in detail.

| 내용구성하기 | | |
|---|---|---|
| Introduction | ☑ 자주 가는 식당의 이름과 장소 | |
| Body | ☑ 식당의 외부 묘사  ☑ 식당의 내부 묘사 | ☑ 좋아하는 이유 |
| Closing | ☑ 추천하기 | |

### Introduction

❶ **One restaurant I really enjoy is** the Mill Street Grill. It ❷ **is located close to my university in Seoul**, so it has been my favorite since my college days.

### Body

It is in a 3-story building. A big parking lot is located right in front of the building. There is a huge sign on the street, so you can't miss it.

Once you go inside, you can see magnificent chandeliers on the ceiling. The ❸ **decor** is classic with comfortable leather chairs. ❹ **It gives the impression that** the restaurant has been successful for many years.

From the food to the ambience, everything about Mill Street Grill is perfect. Not to mention convenient valet parking is available in its huge parking lot.

### Closing

If you have time, I recommend eating at the Mill Street Grill. I'm sure you will love it.

### Useful Expressions

❶ One (location) I really enjoy is...
이름 내가 좋아하는 (장소)는 ~이다.
▶ One restaurant I really enjoy is the Mill Street Grill.

❷ Be located in (location)
(장소)에 위치하다. (located 대신에 situated/placed 사용 가능)
▶ It is located in the center of Seoul.

❸ Decor
인테리어보다 좀더 맥락에 맞는 단어
▶ The owners have put much thought into the decor.

❹ It gives the impression that...
이곳은 나에게 ~인상을 준다.
▶ It gives the impression that the restaurant has been successful for many years.

# IM2  IM3+

| | | IM2 | IM3+ |
|---|---|---|---|
| Introduction | | My favorite restaurant is the Mill Street Grill. | One restaurant I really enjoy is the Mill Street Grill. It is located close to my university in Seoul, so it has been my favorite since my college days. |
| Body | 외부 묘사 | The Mill Street Grill is in a building and there is a big parking lot. | It is in a 3-story building. A big parking lot is located right in front of the building. There is a huge sign on the street, so you can't miss it. |
| | 내부 묘사 | Big chandeliers are on the ceiling and there are nice chairs and other expensive pieces of furniture. | Once you go inside, you can see magnificent chandeliers on the ceiling. The decor is classic with comfortable leather chairs. It gives the impression that the restaurant has been successful for many years. |
| | 좋아하는 이유 | I like its food and there is a big parking lot, so it is convenient to park. | From the food to the ambience, everything about Mill Street Grill is perfect. Not to mention convenient valet parking is available in its huge parking lot. |
| Closing | | It is my favorite restaurant. | If you have time, I recommend eating at the Mill Street Grill. I'm sure you will love it. |

IM1 IM2 ▶ IM3+

### Why IM1~IM2?

① **My favorite restaurant is** 와 같은 be 동사를 사용하는 단순한 형태의 문형
   ▶ 관계 대명사를 포함한 다양한 문장 형태와 일반 동사를 사용해서 대응하세요.

② 주로 묘사 할 때 **there is/are**를 사용하는 답변
   ▶ 다양한 형태의 묘사 문장을 사용하세요.

③ 전체적으로 짧은 답변
   ▶ 외부나 내부, 그리고 이유를 좀 더 자세히 설명함으로써 답변의 길이 조정하세요.

**Q2.** Think of a park in your city that you like to go to. Where is it located? What is the name of the park? What kind of facilities are there? What can you see there? Why do you like to go to the park? Describe the park you like to visit in detail.

**내용구성하기**

| | | |
|---|---|---|
| Introduction | ☑ 좋아하는 공원의 이름과 장소 | |
| Body | ☑ 공원에 대한 정보  ☑ 공원 내부 묘사  ☑ 좋아하는 이유 | |
| Closing | ☑ 추천하기 | |

### Introduction

The park I like to go to best is the Han River Park. It is located close to my home, making it easy to stop by in my spare time.

### Body

It ❶ **was designed to** suit the interests of a wide range of people, and it offers various facilities and attractions.

Because it follows the river, there is ample space. At the entrance of the park that is closest to my house, you can find an area for picnics in addition to swimming pools, which are open in the summer. Bicycle paths and walking trails ❷ **are placed along** the river. Other parts of the park even have fields and courts for different sports.

Compared to other city parks in my community, the Han River Park has ❸ **far more** facilities and offers better views. The convenient location is just one more reason for me to visit the park. I only need to walk 5 minutes to get there. For these reasons, I choose to visit the Han River Park in my free time.

### Closing

If you have time, you should visit the Han River Park and ❹ **take advantage of** its facilities.

### Useful Expressions

❶ Be designed to +V
(동사) 하도록 만들어지다.
▶ It's designed to be very sturdy.

❷ Be placed along (location)
(장소)를 따라 위치하다.
▶ The cards will be placed along side the fireplace.

❸ Far more
훨씬 비교급 한
▶ The park has far more facilities than the picnic area.

❹ Take advantage of A
A를 이용하다.
▶ It's a good idea to take advantage of the good weather.

**Q3.** You indicated in your survey that you live with your family. I would like you to tell me about your house. Where do you live? Where is it located? What does it look like? What do you like about your house? Describe your house as much as you can.

| 내용구성하기 | Introduction | ☑ 내가 사는 집 소개 | | |
|---|---|---|---|---|
| | Body | ☑ 집의 외부 묘사 | ☑ 집의 내부 설명 | ☑ 집을 좋아하는 이유 |
| | Closing | ☑ 느낌 및 의견 | | |

### Introduction

I am currently living in an apartment in the heavily populated city of Seoul.

### Body

I live on the 15th floor of a 25-story building, which is ❶ **in the middle of** a large apartment complex. A small stream and a park are located nearby my apartment. There are two bus stops ❷ **within 5 minutes walking distance**.

When you walk into my house, ❸ **the first thing you can see is** a picture of my family at the end of the hallway. Two doors can be found on the right. One of them is a bathroom and the other is my study.

As you walk down the hallway, a living room and a kitchen are located on either side of the hall. You can see the master bedroom besides the kitchen. I do not have a lot of furniture, only the things that are necessary. I do not clean my house every day but I try to keep it as clean as possible.

Out of all the houses I have lived in, I like my current home the best. It is not only conveniently located near bus stops but also ❹ **situated near** the park. You can enjoy comfortable city life at the same time as beautiful trees.

### Closing

I am very satisfied with my house and I hope to live in it as long as I can.

**Useful Expressions**

❶ In the middle of...
~사이에
▶ It is in the middle of Seoul.

❷ Within (number) minutes walking distance
(숫자)분 안에 걸어갈 수 있는 거리에
▶ She lives within 5 minutes walking distance from the station.

❸ The first thing you can see is...
네가 처음 볼 수 있는 것은 ~이다.
▶ The first thing you can see in the long hallway.

❹ Be situated near...
~근처에 위치해 있다.
▶ The school is situated near the park.

 **My Answer** — Use the expressions from the Key Information to develop your sentences.

- Introduction

- Body

- Closing

# UNIT 4

# 경험 말하기

OPIc 공략! IM3+

# UNIT 04 경험 말하기

**OPIc 공략! IM3+**

## Learning Objectives

본인이 경험한 에피소드에 대해 당시 상황이 언제, 어디에서, 누구와, 무엇이, 어떻게, 왜 (5W1H) 일어났는지, 그리고 그 사건이 기억에 남는 이유와 그 사건으로부터 받은 영향에 대해 말할 수 있다.

## Frequently Asked Questions

- Have you ever had a memorable experience while you went to a movie?
- Did you have any experience of inconvenience due to technical difficulties?
- When was the last time you went on a trip? Where did you go? What did you do?
- Do you remember the first time you became interested in listening to music? Who influenced you?

## Brainstorming

**Step 1** Brainstorm key words and expressions about the topic.
**Step 2** Use the words and expressions to brainstorm possible questions.

**Experience**

- **Recent/Last/Latest Experience**
  Q. When was the last time you went to (a location)?

- **Memorable Experience**
  Q. Do you have any memorable experiences?

- **First Experience**
  Q. Do you remember the first time you went to do (smthing)?

# Key Information

### 시간, 장소, 사람

_____ ago, I went to 장소, with 사람.
전에 나는 장소에 사람과 갔다.

When I was _____, I went to _____.
내가 _____였을 때, _____에 갔다.

▶ 언제 어디서 일어난 일인지 답변 앞부분에 서술하면 경험의 신빙성이 높아 보이는 효과가 있다.
When 주어 동사 구문과 ...ago가 가장 광범위하게 쓰이는 과거 관련 표현이다.

### 사건: 발생 - 고조 - 결과

Suddenly something happened.
갑자기 무슨 일이 생겼다.

I had an unexpected incident.
예기치 못한 사고가 있었다.

It was a little difficult to _____ but _____.
_____ 하기가 좀 어려웠지만 _____.

The greatest thing about it is _____.
가장 멋졌던 점은 _____.

### 느낌이나 생각

After that, I always _____.
그 일 이후 나는 항상 _____ 한다.

Whenever I think of it, I still feel _____.
그 일을 생각할 때마다 나는 여전히 _____을 느낀다.

Since then, I like/hate to _____.
그때 이후로 나는 _____ 하는걸 좋아/싫어한다.

▶ 느낌이나 생각
I always remember my friends who were there with me.
I still feel excited and amazed.
* like/hate은 뒤에 to부정사 혹은 동명사 모두 올 수 있다.
I like/hate to go to a park/going to a park.

OPIc 시험에 가장 비중을 많이 차지하는 문제 유형입니다. 경험은 과거시제를 사용하는 것이 가장 중요한 문법적 요소입니다. 스토리텔링에 많은 평가 기준을 두고 있으니 여러 종류의 이야기와 경험을 준비하는 것이 필요합니다.

## How to Answer

**Q1.** You indicated in your survey that you often go jogging. Have you ever had a special experience when you went jogging? When and where did you go? What happened and what did you do? Tell me why it was so special to you in detail.

**내용구성하기**
- **Introduction** ☑ 기억 남는 경험 소개
- **Body** ☑ 경험이 일어난 시기와 장소  ☑ 정체불명의 물체 발견  ☑ 반전의 결과
- **Closing** ☑ 사건 후의 느낌이나 생각

### Introduction

Every morning, I go to the park alone, but a very strange thing happened one day.

### Body

❶ **About 3 months ago, I went jogging at a park** that I usually go to alone.

❷ **Out of nowhere**, I saw a huge brown animal running towards me. I thought it was a wild animal since I had heard they sometimes have incidents there.

Because I felt very scared, I turned around and started to run in the opposite direction as fast as I could, but the animal was faster. I could feel it coming closer to me. Then I saw it running beside me. I stopped and laughed.

It was just a dog, a really cute one. I was relieved but ❸ **at the same time** felt silly.

### Closing

Whenever I go to that park now, I think about my very special run with the dog.

### Useful Expressions

❶ About (time) ago, I went to (location)
(시간) 전 쯤에 (장소)에 갔다.
▶ About a week ago, I went to the theater.

❷ As (adjective) as I could
가능한 (형용사) 하다.
▶ I ran as fast as I could.

❸ at the same time
동시에
▶ We were hired at the same time.

# IM2  IM3+

| | | IM2 | IM3+ |
|---|---|---|---|
| **Introduction** | | I will tell you about my experience. | Every morning, I go to the park alone, but a very strange thing happened one day. |
| **Body** | 시간과 장소 | I went jogging alone 3 months ago. | About 3 months ago, I went jogging at a park that I usually go to alone. |
| | 사건 발생 (발견) | Suddenly I saw a big animal. It was running towards me. I was scared and ran away. | Out of nowhere, I saw a huge brown animal running towards me. I thought it was a wild animal since I had heard they sometimes have incidents there. |
| | 행동 및 느낌 점 | But the animal ran really fast and it came very close to me, so I could see the animal. | Because I felt very scared, I turned around and started to run in the opposite direction as fast as I could, but the animal was faster. I could feel it coming closer to me. Then I saw it running beside me. I stopped and laughed. |
| | 반전의 결과 | It was a big dog. I felt like a fool. | It was just a dog, a really cute one. I was relieved but at the same time felt silly. |
| **Closing** | | It was a very special experience. | Whenever I go to that park now, I think about my very special run with the dog. |

# Level Up⁺

### Why IM1~IM2?

**01** I will tell you about my experience... 와 같은 1차원 적인 간결한 서론과 결론
▶ 일상을 소개하는 문장과 경험을 소개하는 문장으로 변형해보세요.

**02** 사건의 기술을 단문을 주로 사용한 간단한 형태의 문장과 등위 접속사만을 사용한 답변
▶ 다양한 문장의 형태를 사용하고 종속접속사를 활용한 답변을 구성해보세요.

**03** 사건을 시간 순서대로 서술만 한 짧은 답변
▶ 사건을 좀더 개연성 있게 구성함으로써 문장의 수와 답변의 길이를 늘려보세요.

## Q2.
Have you ever had something unexpected happen when you were shopping? Where did you go? What happened and what did you do? Tell me about your unexpected experience in as much detail as possible.

**내용구성하기**

| | | |
|---|---|---|
| Introduction | ☑ 예상하지 못했던 경험 소개 | |
| Body | ☑ 경험이 일어난 시기와 장소 | ☑ 친구와 식품점 방문 |
| | ☑ 예상치 못한 사건 발생 | ☑ 사건의 원인과 결과 |
| Closing | ☑ 사건 후의 느낌이나 생각 | |

### Introduction

Most people do not think of grocery shopping as particularly exciting, but the strangest thing happened to me when I was in college.

### Body

One summer day, I was going to the grocery store with my roommate.

❶ **On the way to** the store, he had been complaining about a stomachache. It was unusual for him because he was a guy who liked to ❷ **brag about** how much he could bear pain. Once we got to the store, we split up because we needed to buy different things.

While I was looking at notebooks, I heard my name being called on the intercom. Someone was asking me to come to the entrance of the store. As I ❸ **made my way to the front of the store**, I spotted my roommate being wheeled out on a stretcher.

Apparently, his stomachache was appendicitis, and he was being transported to the hospital for emergency surgery. Fortunately, he recovered quickly.

### Closing

That was one very special experience at a grocery store. Have you ever had a strange experience shopping, Eva?

**Useful Expressions**

❶ On the way to...
~가는 중에
▶ On the way to the store, I met him.

❷ Brag about
자랑하다, 거들먹거리다.
▶ He likes to brag about his son.

❸ Make one's way to A
A로 나아가다, 가다
▶ I made my way to the store.

**Q3.** Have you had any unforgettable experiences while you were traveling? When and where did you go? Who did you go with? What happened? Why do you think it was an unforgettable experience? Tell me about it in as much detail as possible.

내용구성하기

| | | |
|---|---|---|
| Introduction | ☑ 처음 경험 소개 | |
| Body | ☑ 경험이 일어난 시기와 장소 | ☑ 여행 관련 조언들 ☑ 릭쇼를 탄 원인 |
| | ☑ 불안한 사건 발생 | ☑ 반전 결과 |
| Closing | ☑ 사건 후의 느낌이나 생각 | |

### Introduction

Listening to the questions you asked, my trip to India is the ❶ **first thing that comes to mind**.

### Body

I planned the trip for about a year before finally going to India by myself.

Before the trip I heard warnings about traveling alone, advising travelers to be careful around strangers, and to avoid dark, secluded alleys. I ❷ **was fully aware of** the dangers.

My story starts on a very hot day in India. I wanted to drink a glass of icy cold beer but it was hard to find somewhere to go since very few restaurants and bars ❸ **are licensed to** sell alcohol. Finally I took an auto-rickshaw to find a restaurant that served beer around dusk.

The rickshaw driver told me he knew of the perfect place. Ten minutes later, I noticed that I was getting farther and farther from the familiar part of town. It was getting dark quickly. I asked the driver to turn around but he did not seem to understand me.

Just as I started to panic, a spacious garden appeared in front of us and I was able to enjoy a nice beer at a lovely restaurant.

### Closing

From this experience, I learned that sometimes it is best just to relax and trust that everything will work out.

**Useful Expressions**

❶ First thing that comes to mind
가장 먼저 떠오르는 것
▸ It was the first thing that came to my mind.

❷ Be aware of...
~을 알다, 알아차리다
▸ She must be aware of the consequences.

❸ Be licensed to +V
(동사원형)하는 것이 허락되다.
▸ The store was licensed to sell beer.

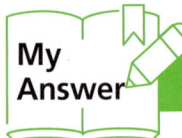

**My Answer** — Use the expressions from the Key Information to develop your sentences.

- Introduction

- Body

- Closing

# UNIT 5

## OPIc 공략! IM3+

### 비교하기

# UNIT 05 비교하기

OPIc 공략! IM3+

## Learning Objectives

두 가지 각 각의 외관, 기능 및 역할, 특징 등을 설명하고, 서로 같거나 다른 점을 비교하여 말할 수 있다.

## Frequently Asked Questions

- I would like you to compare the house you used to live in and the house that you are living in now.
- Please tell me about two singers or musicians that you like.
- Could you tell me about some similarities and differences between two movies that you like?
- Have you noticed any changes between traveling in the past and traveling now?
- Tell me about some changes that have occurred in banks. Compare the past and the present.

## Brainstorming

**Step 1** Brainstorm key words and expressions about the topic.
**Step 2** Use the words and expressions to brainstorm possible questions.

**House**
Q. What are some differences between your previous house and your current house?

**Music Gadget**
Q. Have you noticed any changes between music gadgets in the past and those in the present?

**Comparisons and Changes**

**Recycling**
Q. Tell me about how the recycling system your country used in past differs from the one it uses today.

**Community (Neighborhood)**
Q. Have there been any changes in your community over the years?

## Key Information

### 과거와 현재

I have noticed some changes in _____.
_____ 에서 약간의 변화들을 알아챘다.

There are several differences between _____ and _____.
_____ 와 _____ 에는 몇 가지 차이점이 있다.

▶ 과거와 현재를 비교하는 것이므로 현재 완료를 사용하여 현재까지도 그 변화를 체감하고 있음을 표현 하는 것도 좋다.

### 비교하기

It is much/even 비교급 than _____.
그것은 _____ 보다 훨씬 (비교급)하다.

It is as 형용사/부사 as _____.
그것은 _____ 만큼 (형용사/부사) 하다.

▶ 비교급은 단순 비교와 원급 비교등이 있다.
단순비교 A가 B보다 ~하다.
A 형용사/부사+(e)r than B
A more 형용사/부사 than B
원급비교 A는 B만큼 ~하다.
A as 형용사/부사 as B.

### 다른점 말하기

I used to 동사.
나는 예전에 (동사)하곤 했다.

A different thing about _____ is _____.
_____ 의 다른 점은 _____ 이다.

What I like about _____ is _____.
_____ 에서 좋아하는 점은 _____ 이다.

_____ is different from _____.
_____ 는 _____ 와 다르다.

### Answer tips!

과거시제와 현재시제의 정확한 사용으로 의도하는 내용을 명확하게 전달하는 것이 중요합니다. 과거에는 단순 두 개의 장소나 사물, 사람 등을 비교하는 문제가 많이 나왔으며 최근에도 출제될 가능성이 있지만 선택하는 난이도가 올라갈수록 단순 비교보다는 과거와 현재의 변화를 설명하라는 문제들이 더 많이 출제되고 있습니다.

## How to Answer

**Q1.** I would like you to tell me about the house you are currently living in and then compare it to a house you lived in before. What are some differences? Are those differences better or worse? Please compare the two houses in as much detail as possible.

| 내용구성하기 | | |
|---|---|---|
| Introduction | ☑ 과거의 집과 현재의 집 차이점 소개 | |
| Body | ☑ 과거의 집 묘사와 장점 | ☑ 과거의 집 단점 |
| | ☑ 현재의 집 묘사와 장점 | ☑ 현재의 집 단점 |
| Closing | ☑ 느낌 및 의견 | |

### Introduction

There are many differences between the house I ❶ **used to live in** and my current home.

### Body

I used to live with my parents. ❷ **As far as I can remember**, we moved to more than 5 different houses together. I'd like to describe the last house I lived in with my parents. It was a typical apartment with 4 bedrooms. A good thing about that apartment was that there were a lot of trees nearby, so I could hear birds singing and the air was clean and fresh. Although it was a little far from things, we were all happy to live there.

The house I am currently living in is another typical apartment with 3 bedrooms. It is a little smaller, but not that different from my previous house. However, it is located very close to a subway station. In addition, there is a big shopping mall located nearby my house, so it is very convenient.

### Closing

It is really hard to say which one I like best since ❸ **each house has its own advantages**. I love them all!

### Useful Expressions

❶ Used to +V
(동사원형)하곤 했다.
▶ I used to live in Canada.

❷ As far as I can remember
내 기억으로는
▶ As far as I can remember, there was a strange house nearby.

❸ Has its own advantages
각각의 장점이 있다
▶ Each one has its own advantages.

# IM2  IM3+

| | | IM2 | IM3+ |
|---|---|---|---|
| **Introduction** | | I am going to talk about my last 2 homes. | There are many differences between the house I used to live in and my current home. |
| **Body** | 과거의 집 묘사 | My previous house was an apartment. I lived with my parents. There were 4 bedrooms, a kitchen, a living room and 2 bathrooms. | I used to live with my parents. As far as I can remember, we moved to more than 5 different houses together. I'd like to describe the last house I lived in with my parents. It was a typical apartment with 4 bedrooms. |
| | 과거의 집 장단점 | There were many trees. The air was fresh and I could see birds. | A good thing about that apartment was that there were a lot of trees nearby, so I could hear birds singing and the air was clean and fresh. Although it was a little far from things, we were all happy to live there. |
| | 현재의 집 묘사 | My current home is an apartment, too. There are 3 bedrooms, a kitchen, a living room and 2 bathrooms. | The house I am living currently in is another typical apartment with 3 bedrooms. It is a little smaller, but not that different from my previous house. |
| | 현재의 집 장단점 | There are bus stops and a subway station nearby. A shopping mall is close to my house. | However, it is located very close to a subway station. In addition, there is a big shopping mall located nearby my house, so it is very convenient. |
| **Closing** | | I like both of houses very much. | It is really hard to say which one I like best since each house has its own advantages. I love them all! |

IM1 IM2 ▶ IM3+

### Why IM1~IM2?

**01** 1인칭을 사용한 간결하고 단순한 서론과 결론
▶ 다양한 주어들을 사용한 문장들 사용하며 느낌과 의견을 포함한 서론과 결론을 만들어 보세요.

**02** There is 와 there are의 사용에 치우친 답변. 반복적인 문장 형태 사용
▶ 앞 뒤의 문장을 다른 형태로 사용. 다양한 사실에 초점을 맞추어 집을 설명해보세요.

## Q2. What are the differences between a trip you took in the past and one that you might take in the present? If there are any, please describe the differences in detail.

**내용구성하기**

**Introduction** ☑ 여행 습관의 과거와 현재의 차이점 소개
**Body** ☑ 과거에 어른들과 여행  ☑ 현재엔 친구나 혼자 여행
☑ 과거의 수동적 여행  ☑ 현재의 능동적 여행
**Closing** ☑ 느낌 및 의견

### Introduction

❶ **Ever since** I started traveling alone, I have noticed several changes in my travel habits.

### Body

When I was young, it was always my parents, grandparents, uncles and aunts whom I traveled with. I ❷ **was not allowed to** travel alone or with my friends mainly because I was too young to travel without adults.

As I grew older, I was finally able to go on trips by myself or with my friends. That was the biggest change.

Also, I used to be someone who only had to wait and follow adults' instructions when traveling. I did not need to do anything. I had a very passive role when it came to vacations until several years ago. I had to learn to do things myself.

However, after several learning experiences, I am now such an enthusiastic and active traveler. I do ❸ **not only** plan where to travel, what to see, and where to eat **but I also** pay for my travel expenses by myself.

### Closing

Now, I can truly enjoy traveling anywhere with anybody.

### Useful Expressions

❶ Ever since
~이후로 줄곧, 계속
▶ He had a car ever since he was 18 years old.

❷ Be allowed to...
~하는 것이 허용되다
▶ I was not allowed to sleep late.

❸ Not only A but also B
A뿐만 아니라 B도
▶ He is not only poor but also lazy.

**Q3.** Have you noticed any changes in your city's transportation system? What are some changes you have seen? Are all the changes improvements? Tell me about some of the changes in as much detail as possible.

**내용구성하기**

| | | |
|---|---|---|
| **Introduction** | ☑ | 과거와 현재의 교통의 변화 소개 |
| **Body** | ☑ | 과거 유동인구 부족으로 대중교통시설 미비 |
| | ☑ | 현재 편리하게 갖춰진 대중교통시설 |
| **Closing** | ☑ | 느낌 및 의견 |

### Introduction

I am ❶ **not an expert on** my city's public transportation system but I have noticed some changes.

### Body

When I moved to the city about 10 years ago, it was little difficult to take public transportation. It was a new city, so the roads were great! They were wide, clean, and there was even a shortcut to get to the highway.

Since there were not many people living there, buses did not run often and the subway station was still under the construction. It was ❷ **the perfect place for** people with their own cars to live.

Recently, the situation has changed from what it was 10 years ago. The construction of the subway station has been completed and a new express train station was built, so I can reach anywhere in Korea in 4 hours or less. Many more bus lines are running and multiple bus stops are located in front of my home.

### Closing

I think ❸ **things have changed for the better**, so people in my city are able to live more conveniently than before.

### Useful Expressions

❶ Not an expert on(in)
~에 전문가가 아니다
▶ I am not an expert on marketing.

❷ The perfect place for...
~하기에 (~에게) 완벽한 장소
▶ It was the perfect place for traveling.

❸ Things have changed for the better
상황이 호전되고 있다
▶ Things have changed for the better in this country.

 **My Answer** — Use the expressions from the Key Information to develop your sentences.

— Introduction

— Body

— Closing

# OPIc
## 공략! IM3+

UNIT 6

이슈(Issue) 묻기

# UNIT 06

## 이슈(Issue) 묻기

OPIc 공략! IM3+

### Learning Objectives

어떤 일이나 활동에 대해 문제점을 제기하고 느낌 및 의견을 말할 수 있다.

### Frequently Asked Questions

- Are there any issues or concerns regarding buying or renting a house in your country?
- Are there any environmental concerns that people may have regarding trekking or hiking?
- Expert says it is important to have a vacation. What do you think about this?
- There might be some issues or concerns in your neighborhood(community). What are some issues?

### Brainstorming

**Step 1** Brainstorm key words and expressions about the topic.
**Step 2** Use the words and expressions to brainstorm possible questions.

**Issues and Concerns**

**Music Devices**
Q. Tell me some issues or concerns regarding music devices.

**Technology**
Q. Can you think of any issues or concerns related to technology usage?

**Trekking/Hiking**
Q. Can you think of any issues or concerns related to trekking?

**Food**
Q. Have you heard about any issues related to water or food shortages around the world?

# Key Information

### 문제제기

There has been an issue or a concern related to _____.
　　　　와 관련해서 문제점이나 이슈가 있습니다.

People are talking about _____.
　　　　가 사람들 사이에서 화제입니다.

_____ is a hot issue recently.
_____가 최근 이슈입니다.

The main concern or issue is _____.
주요 문제 또는 이슈는 _____.

▶ Due to는 because of 와 마찬가지로 구를 목적으로 수반하는 표현. 즉 뒤에 주어 동사를 포함한 절의 형태가 나오는 because랑은 의미는같지만 문법적 사용이 다른 표현

### 문제점들

Due to _____, it became damaged.
_____때문에 손해를 입었습니다.

There are not enough _____.
_____가 부족합니다.

It is getting dangerous/difficult/uncomfortable to _____.
_____하기가 위험해지고/어려워지고/불편해지고 있습니다.

_____ makes it contaminated/dirty.
_____로 인해 오염/더러워졌습니다.

### 느낌 및 의견

I personally consider _____.
개인적으로 _____라고 생각합니다

I believe that _____.
전 _____라고 생각합니다.

It is worth _____.
_____할만한 가치가 있습니다.

The society should reconsider _____.
사회에서 _____를 재고해야 합니다.

People need to _____.
사람들은 _____할 필요가 있습니다.

## Answer tips!

주로 난이도 5이상 15번 문제로 출제됩니다. 어렵거나 전문적인 지식을 물어보는 문제라고 느껴질 수 있는데 실제 응시자들을 당황시키는 데 더 큰 의도를 가지고 있습니다. 전문적이거나 어려운 이슈 또는 문제점을 제시하기 보다는 주위에서 쉽게 생각할 수 있는 것들에 초점을 맞춰 답변을 구성해야 합니다. 최근에는 의견을 물어보는 유형의 문제도 나오고 있으니 주의하세요.

## How to Answer

**Q1.** There might be some issues or concerns in your neighborhood or community. What are some recent issues? What do you think about them? Can you think of any way to resolve the issues? Tell me about them with details.

| 내용구성하기 | | |
|---|---|---|
| Introduction | ☑ 문제 제기 | |
| Body | ☑ 망가진 길의 문제점 | ☑ 어두운 길의 문제점 |
| | ☑ 문제를 해결하기 위한 노력 | |
| Closing | ☑ 느낌 및 의견 | |

### Introduction

There have been some issues in my neighborhood recently. Many people are talking about how to improve a walking path along a narrow stream.

### Body

There is already a walking path, which ❶ **is supposed to** provide a shortcut to the community center but it is old and damaged. Even for adults, it is difficult to walk on, so people have to make a much longer detour.

In addition, at night, it is ❷ **too dark to walk on** because there are not enough streetlamps. As a result, it is dangerous for people to enjoy the path in the evening and actually, there have been several minor offences, such as vandalism.

Now, local residents are ❸ **in the process of filing** a petition asking for the path to be improved. I am part of the group organizing the petition and it is almost done.

### Closing

I believe that improvement in any way is necessary and whoever is in charge should consider this matter seriously.

### Useful Expressions

❶ Be supposed to...
~하기로 되어있다
▸ I was supposed to do my homework.

❷ Too … to …
너무 ~해서 ~할 수 없다.
▸ I was too young to drive.

❸ Be in the process of -ing
~하는 중이다
▸ They are in the process of filing a petition.

# IM2 vs IM3+

| | | IM2 | IM3+ |
|---|---|---|---|
| Introduction | | There is an issue about a walking road in my neighborhood. | There have been some issues in my neighborhood recently. Many people are talking about how to improve a walking path along a narrow stream. |
| Body | 문제점 1 (망가진 길) | There is an old walking road but it is not good. So people do not use it and have to go to a different road. | There is already a walking path, which is supposed to provide a shortcut to the community center, but it is old and damaged. Even for adults, it is difficult to walk on, so people have to make a much longer detour. |
| | 문제점 2 (어두운 길) | It is a longer way and at night, it is not safe. Because it is very dark, it can be dangerous to go there. | In addition, at night, it is too dark to walk on because there are not enough streetlamps. As a result, it is dangerous for people to enjoy the path in the evening and actually, there have been several minor offences, such as vandalism. |
| | 해결하기 위한 노력 | So now people are asking for the road to be repaired. | Now, local residents are in the process of filing a petition asking for the path to be improved. I am part of the group organizing the petition and it is almost done. |
| Closing | | I hope it will be better soon. | I believe that improvement in any way is necessary and whoever is in charge should consider this matter seriously. |

## Level Up+

IM1 IM2 ▶ IM3+

### Why IM1~IM2?

**01** Road처럼 길이란 의미는 같지만 산책로에는 잘 사용하지 않는 미묘한 차이가 있는 단어 사용
  ▶ road를 밟아 만든길 이라는 의미를 가진 path로 바꿔보세요.

**02** 단문들로만 연결된 사건서술 문장들
  ▶ 서로 다른 형태의 중문과 장문을 다양한 접속사로 연결하여 사건들을 좀 더 짜임새 있게 연결해보세요.

**Q2.** Can you think of any environmental concerns or issues that people may have regarding hiking and trekking? If there are, please tell me about them and their potential solutions.

**내용구성하기**

| | | |
|---|---|---|
| **Introduction** | ☑ 문제와 연관된 영화 소개 | |
| **Body** | ☑ 영화에서 본 많은 사람들의 트래킹 모습 | ☑ 쓰레기 급증 |
| | ☑ 쓰레기에 의존하는 야생동물 | |
| **Closing** | ☑ 느낌 및 의견 | |

### Introduction

A few months ago, I watched a movie called The Himalayas.

### Body

The first scene of the movie really shocked me. It showed the base of a mountain with a number of people waiting in a long line for their turn to hike up. The movie briefly mentioned that there are concerns ❶ **due to** an increasing number of people visiting the mountain.

From the movie, I realized that there might be serious environmental issues related to hiking and trekking. As the number of people trekking grows, tons of waste is left behind. Although ❷ **there have been efforts to** reduce and recover waste, too many people are trekking the mountain. The waste not only contaminates the mountain itself, but also wild animals living in the mountain come to depend on it as a food source, so they may lose their natural instincts.

### Closing

It will be difficult to fix this problem immediately but it seems clear that trekkers need ❸ **to pay extra attention to** the environment and the nature they enjoy.

**Useful Expressions**

❶ Due to...
~때문에
▸ Due to the cold weather, we couldn't go on a picnic.

❷ There have been efforts to...
~하기 위한 노력이 있다.
▸ There have been efforts to cut down on greenhouse gases.

❸ Pay attention to...
~에 주목하다, ~에 유의하다
▸ We need to pay attention to the environment.

**Q3.** Some experts say that vacations are necessary. Do you believe going on vacation is necessary too? If you do, why do you feel that way?

| 내용구성하기 | Introduction | ☑ 개인 의견 제시 |
| --- | --- | --- |
| | Body | ☑ 삶의 질을 개선하는 의미에서 휴가의 필요성 |
| | | ☑ 개인의 성장의 의미에서 휴가의 필요성 |
| | Closing | ☑ 느낌 및 의견 |

### Introduction

I totally ❶ **agree with** the experts' opinion about vacations.

### Body

I think that vacations are necessary for people for several reasons. First, they can improve the quality of our everyday lives. What I mean is that many people plan their vacations in advance and feel good about them until the date comes. When thinking about their upcoming vacations, they are able to do whatever they need to do even when they face difficulties. A vacation can help them ❷ **get through** everyday life.

Second, I think vacations open a new opportunity for personal development. People ❸ **are likely to** be exposed to unexpected and different situations in places they are not familiar with and by dealing with these issues, they can grow as people.

### Closing

Therefore, I think vacations are essential. What I think might not always be right but I am pretty sure that there will be more people who agree with me on this topic than those who don't.

### Useful Expressions

❶ Agree with...
~에 동의하다
▶ I agree with your opinion.

❷ Get through
지나오다, 헤어나오다, 합격하다
▶ He helped me get through the college.

❸ Be likely to...
개연성이 있다, ~할 것 같다
▶ People are likely to be exposed to difficult situations.

**My Answer** — Use the expressions from the Key Information to develop your sentences.

— Introduction




— Body




— Closing

# 실력다지기

## ☑ Part 2 설문주제

**Unit 7** | 영화/TV 보기
**Unit 8** | 쇼핑하기
**Unit 9** | 공연/콘서트 보기
**Unit 10** | 공원/캠핑 가기
**Unit 11** | 음악 감상하기
**Unit 12** | 요리하기
**Unit 13** | 조깅/걷기
**Unit 14** | 하이킹/ 트레킹
**Unit 15** | 국내/해외 여행
**Unit 16** | 집에서 휴가 보내기

# OPIc 공략! IM3+

# OPIc
공략! IM3+

## UNIT 7
### 영화/TV 보기

# UNIT 07

## 영화/TV 보기

OPIc 공략! IM3+

### Learning Objectives

좋아하는 영화나 TV프로그램의 내용, 배우, 기억에 남는 내용 등에 관해 말할 수 있다.

### Frequently Asked Questions

- What types of movies/TV programs do you like to watch? Why do you like to watch them?
- Describe a place you usually go to watch movies.
- Describe an actor or an actress/TV star.
- Tell me what you usually do before or after watching a movie.
- Do you have a memorable or recent experience watching a movie?

### Brainstorming

**Step 1** Brainstorm key words and expressions about the topic.
**Step 2** Use the words and expressions to brainstorm possible questions.

**Stars**
Q. Who is your favorite star?

**Movie or TV Program**
Q. Which movie do you like the most?

**Movies and TV**

**Experience**
Q. Have you ever had a special experience watching a movie?

**Movie Theater**
Q. Tell me about the movie theater you usually go to.

# Key Information

### 영화/TV 프로그램

The movie was released last Friday.
그 영화는 지난 주 금요일에 개봉했습니다.

The show has been on TV for 5 years.
그 쇼는 5년간 TV방영 중입니다.

It is based on a true story.
그 이야기는 실화에 근거했습니다.

▶ 영화가 개봉하다 라는 표현 open과 be released 둘 다 사용 가능하다.

### 배우/여배우

The actor/actress appears to be _____.
그 배우/여배우는 _____ 해 보여요.

He/She speaks out about _____.
그/그녀는 _____ 에 대해 얘기했습니다.

▶ Appear
자동사로 바로 명사의 형태가 올 수 없으며 in, on 등과 같은 전치사나 to 부정사가 사용된다.

### 극장

Once you go in, you cannot miss the _____ right in front of you.
극장에 들어가면 바로 앞에 있는 _____ 가 보입니다.

_____ is there for people's convenience.
관객 편의를 위해 _____ 가 있습니다.

### 활동

I have an app for booking movie tickets installed on my phone.
제 휴대폰엔 영화티켓 예약용 앱이 설치되어 있습니다.

I can check the timetable to see when the movies are showing.
영화 시간표를 확인할 수 있습니다.

▶ Installed는 생략될 수 있는 관계대명사와 be동사 구문 which(that) is 가 생략된 문장의 형식이다.
Ticket which(that) is installed... 가 원래 형태

특정한 프로그램에 대해서 묘사하는 문제입니다. 프로그램의 내용과 특징 그리고 좋아하는 이유 등이 세부적으로 묘사되어야 합니다.

## How to Answer

**Q1.** You indicated in your survey that you like to watch TV. What is your favorite TV program? What genre is it, and what is the main idea of the program? Please tell me about the program, and describe why you like it in detail.

| 내용구성하기 | | |
|---|---|---|
| Introduction | ☑ 가장 좋아하는 TV 프로그램 소개 | |
| Body | ☑ 반영 기간   ☑ 프로그램의 내용 | ☑ 좋아하는 이유 |
| Closing | ☑ 느낌 및 의견 | |

### Introduction

The TV show I like to watch most is the American TV series *Criminal Minds*.

### Body

The show has been on TV for more than a decade and this is proof of how popular the program is.

The show is mainly about a team of FBI agents. Most of their cases involve analyzing criminal behavior and predicting the thoughts and actions of criminals. This ❶ **is referred to as** "profiling". The agents are also called profilers. They set about catching various criminals through behavioral profiling. The show focuses not only on the team working the cases but also on their personal lives.

The most shocking thing about the show is that a lot of the stories ❷ **are based on** true cases. This is the main reason I like the show. It is realistic and the charming characters are just another reason why I love to watch it.

### Closing

If you have not watched it, I would recommend this show to you. You ❸ **won't regret it**.

**Useful Expressions**

❶ Be referred to as...
~로 불리다
▶ I was referred to as "big sister".

❷ Be based on...
~에 기초하다, 근거하다
▶ It was based on true stories

❸ Won't regret it
후회하지 않을 것이다
▶ You won't regret it.

★ 특정한 프로그램에 대해서 묘사하는 문제입니다. 프로그램의 내용과 특징 그리고 좋아하는 이유 등이 세부적으로 묘사되어야 합니다.

# IM2  vs IM3+

| | | IM2 | IM3+ |
|---|---|---|---|
| **Introduction** | | My favorite show's name is Criminal Minds. | The TV show I like to watch most is the American TV series Criminal Minds. |
| **Body** | 프로그램 반영 기간 | It is a popular American drama. | The show has been on TV for more than a decade and this is proof of how popular the program is. |
| | 프로그램 내용 | There are FBI agents and they try to find criminals. This is the special thing about the show. They use people's behavior to catch criminals. | The show is mainly about a team of FBI agents. Most of their cases involve analyzing criminal behavior and predicting the thoughts and actions of criminals. This is referred to as "profiling". The agents are also called profilers. They set about catching various criminals through behavioral profiling. The show focuses not only on the team working the cases but also on their personal lives. |
| | 좋아하는 이유 | Also, most of the stories are true stories. It was really shocking to me. | The most shocking thing about the show is that a lot of the stories are based on true cases. This is the main reason I like the show. It is realistic and the charming characters are just another reason why I love to watch it. |
| **Closing** | | It is my favorite TV program. | If you have not watched it, I would recommend this show to you. You won't regret it. |

## Level Up+

IM1  IM2  ▶  **IM3+**

### Why IM1~IM2?

**01** My favorite show's name 와 같은 소유격은 어색하고 한국식 표현임
　▶ the show I like... 또는 the name of the show 로 전환해보세요.

**02** American drama에서 드라마는 프로그램의 한 종류를 의미하는 것이지 한글의 드라마와는 의미가 조금 다름
　▶ show나 program으로 바꾸어서 서술해보세요.

**03** 단문들로만 연결된 사건서술 문장들
　▶ 서로 다른 형태의 중문과 장문을 다양한 접속사로 연결하여 사건들을 좀 더 짜임새 있게 연결하세요.

**Q2.** What do you usually do before watching movies? Tell me about all the activities you do before watching movies from beginning to end.

**내용구성하기**
- **Introduction** ☑ 영화보기 전 행동들 소개
- **Body** ☑ 영화 결정  ☑ 영화 티켓 예매  ☑ 영화관 도착 후 한 일
- **Closing** ☑ 느낌 및 의견

### Introduction

As a movie lover, I frequently go to the movies.

### Body

❶ **The first thing I do** before going to the movies is deciding what kind of movie I would like to watch. Since I have an app installed on my phone, so I can check what kinds of movies are showing in theaters, view timetables for movies and even read their reviews. Once I decide which movie I want to watch, I usually reserve a ticket and choose the seat I want with the same application. I could buy a ticket ❷ **in person** but I do not like to wait in line and sometimes I cannot get the seat I want.

After that, I go to the movie theater about 10 minutes before the show starts to buy a bottle of water and then I ❸ **am ready to** watch the movie.

### Closing

This is what I normally do when watching a movie.

### Useful Expressions

❶ The first thing I do
내가 제일 먼저 하는 것
▶ The first thing I do is to check weather.

❷ In person
직접, 스스로
▶ I met him in person.

❸ Be ready to + V
~할 준비가 되다
▶ The first thing I do is to check weather.

★ 활동(activity) 문제로 시간 순서대로, 현재 시제로 답변을 구성하는 것이 좋습니다.
답변이 짧을 경우에는 영화를 본 후에 활동도 첨가해서 답변을 구성하세요.

**Q3.** Do you remember the first time you watched a movie? When was it and whom did you go with? What was the name of the movie? Do you still remember the plot? How did you feel? Tell me about your first movie watching experience in as much detail as possible.

| 내용구성하기 | Introduction | ☑ 처음 영화를 본 시기 | |
|---|---|---|---|
| | Body | ☑ 영화 내용 | ☑ 영화를 본 후 느낌 |
| | Closing | ☑ 나의 의견 | |

### Introduction

As a teenager, I went to the movies with my friends ❶ **for the first time**.

### Body

The movie we saw was Titanic. I was very excited and felt like an adult. Actually, everyone was excited. We went to a big movie theater in the city, and we bought a box of popcorn and three bottles of coke.

Once the movie started, I ❷ **got totally hooked on** the story. It was about the tragic accident of the Titanic and the people on the ship.

Even though I was young then, I could understand why it has become an ❸ **all-time favorite** movie for many people. It was so impressive that my friends and I talked about the movie later while having dinner together.

### Closing

I still remember some lines from the movie and it is still definitely one of my greatest movie going experiences.

### Useful Expressions

❶ For the first time
처음으로
▶ He fell in love for the first time.

❷ Be hooked on…
~에 빠져있다
▶ I was hooked on the movie.

❸ All-time favorite
고전, 매우 좋아하는
▶ The movie is all-time favorite.

★ 첫 영화에 관련된 묘사 문제가 아닌 영화를 처음 본 경험 문제임으로 너무 영화에 대한 설명에 치우치지 않게 주의하세요.

**My Answer** — Use the expressions from the Key Information to develop your sentences.

− Introduction

− Body

− Closing

# OPIc
공략! IM3+

UNIT 8

쇼핑하기

# UNIT 08 쇼핑하기

**OPIc 공략! IM3+**

## Learning Objectives

자주가는 쇼핑 장소에 대해 소개하고 쇼핑패턴 및 쇼핑경험에 대해 이야기 할 수 있다.

## Frequently Asked Questions

- How many hours a week do you usually spend shopping? How often do you go shopping? What kind of items do you generally buy?
- Let's talk about some items that you like to shop for. Describe what you enjoy buying most.
- Please tell me about the places you usually go shopping.
- Do you have any memorable or recent experiences shopping?
- What do you usually do before and after shopping?

## Brainstorming

**Step 1** Brainstorm key words and expressions about the topic.
**Step 2** Use the words and expressions to brainstorm possible questions.

### Place
Q. Describe a shopping mall you like to go to.

### Items
Q. What do you usually buy when you go shopping?

### Shopping

### Experiences
Q. I would like you to tell me about a shopping experience you have had.

### Activities/Habits
Q. Tell you what you usually do before going shopping.

## Key Information

### 쇼핑몰

A wide range of products is available in the stores.
다양한 상품이 상점에 준비되어 있습니다.

On both sides of the hallway, there are _____.
통로 양쪽에는 _____ 들이 있습니다.

▶ Eye shopping vs. Window shopping
Eye shopping으로 알려져 있는 표현은 영어로는 window shipping으로 표현하는 것이 적절하다.

### 활동

I like to look around.
둘러보는 것도 좋아합니다.

I love to window shop before I buy things.
물건을 실제 구입하기 전에 둘러보는 것을 좋아합니다.

Without _____, I cannot _____.
전 _____ 가 없으면 _____ 할 수 없습니다.

▶ Be overcharged가 원래의 표현이며 현재완료의 표현 have been overcharged를 사용함으로써 현재까지도 과다청구당한 상태를 강조 할 수 있다.

### 경험

I have been overcharged for _____.
_____ 로 바가지를 당한 적이 있습니다.

I got ripped off.
바가지를 썼습니다.

In return, I got store credit.
보상으로 상품권을 받았습니다.

▶ Be/get ripped off
바가지씌움을 당하다는 표현이다.

뉴오픽이 도입되면서 자주 출제되는 돌발문제입니다. 쇼핑과 관련해서는 1) 쇼핑패턴 (누구와 언제, 어디에서, 얼마나 자주 쇼핑을 하는지), 2)쇼핑경험 (비용지불 방법 및 환불 경험/ 쇼핑 방식 및 활동), 3) 쇼핑 장소에 대한 묘사 등에 대한 질문들이 출제됩니다. 기본적으로 쇼핑습관 및 구매활동에 대한 답변을 구성해 돌발 상황을 대비해 두는 것이 좋습니다.

## How to Answer

**Q1.** I would like to know what you do before and after shopping. Tell me about your shopping routine from beginning to end.

| 내용구성하기 | Introduction | ☑ 쇼핑일과 및 단계 | |
|---|---|---|---|
| | Body | ☑ 리스트 만들기 | ☑ 가는 방법 |
| | | ☑ 물건 구매 | ☑ 쇼핑 후 하는 일 |
| | Closing | ☑ 느낌 및 의견 | |

### Introduction

❶ **As much as** I like shopping, I take some steps to prevent myself from spending too much.

### Body

Before I go shopping, I write down items I want to buy. Without a list, I might buy things I do not need.

❷ **Once my list is ready**, I go to the store. I usually drive but if I think there might be a lot of cars like on weekends or during the holidays I ❸ **would rather** use public transportation because I hate waiting in the car to find parking.

After arriving at the shopping mall, I first check the locations of stores where I can find the items on my list. It does not take a lot of time to look for the items I need but selecting the right one in the store can ❹ **take a while**.

Once I find everything I planned to buy, I have a cup of coffee and look at what I bought.

### Closing

This is what I usually do when I go shopping.

### Useful Expressions

❶ As much as…
~만큼이나
▶ As much as I like shopping

❷ Once … is ready
~가 준비되면
▶ Once my list is ready, I go to the store.

❸ Would rather…
~하겠다
▶ I would rather go to the movies.

❹ Take a while
시간이 좀 걸린다
▶ It is going to take a while.

# IM2  IM3+

| | | IM2 | IM3+ |
|---|---|---|---|
| **Introduction** | | I will tell you about the activities I usually do before shopping. | As much as I like shopping, I take some steps to prevent myself from spending too much. |
| **Body** | 준비 단계 | First, I make a shopping list. Then I go to the shopping mall. | Before I go shopping, I write down items I want to buy. Without a list, I might buy things I do not need. |
| | 가는 방법 | I always drive or take the subway. | Once my list is ready, I go to the store. I usually drive but if I think there might be a lot of cars like on weekends or during the holidays I would rather use public transportation because I hate waiting in the car to find parking. |
| | 물건 구매 | When I arrive at the mall, I check different stores and buy the things on my list. | After arriving at the shopping mall, I first check the locations of stores where I can find the items on my list. It does not take a lot of time to look for the items I need but selecting the right one in the store can take a while. |
| | 쇼핑 후 하는 일 | After buying everything on the list, I have a cup of coffee and look at those things. | Once I find everything I planned to buy, I have a cup of coffee and look at what I bought. |
| **Closing** | | This is how I shop. | This is what I usually do when I go shopping. |

## Level Up+

### Why IM1~IM2?

**01** 단순히 문제를 반복해서 언급하는 본론과 결론
   ▶ 문제에 언급된 반복되는 단어를 사용하는 대신 다른 형태의 문장으로 답변을 시작하세요.

**02** 주로 하는 행동만을 순서대로 언급
   ▶ 그 행동을 하는 이유도 함께 언급하면서 문장의 수와 길이를 늘려보세요.

## Q2.
Do you have any good or bad experiences from shopping? If so, please tell me when it happened. Where were you? What exactly happened on that day? Tell me about your experience in as much detail as possible.

**내용구성하기**

| | | |
|---|---|---|
| **Introduction** | ✓ 기억에 남는 쇼핑 경험의 장소와 시기 | |
| **Body** | ✓ 불편한 만남 | ✓ 즐거운 경험 |
| **Closing** | ✓ 느낌 및 의견 | |

### Introduction

About 3 weeks ago, right before Korean Thanksgiving Day, I went to a department store located near my mother's house. I needed to buy gifts for some family members and friends.

### Body

❶ **While I was looking** at the cosmetics, suddenly I noticed somebody watching me. I thought it was a misunderstanding but when my eyes met her eyes twice, I realized I was not wrong. I was still feeling uncomfortable when she approached me.

It ❷ **turned out** that she was a friend from my high school. I did not recognize her at first. She looked very ❸ **different from** how I remembered her. Anyway, we were really excited because we had not seen each other for more than 5 years.

After this, we went to a coffee shop and talked a lot. We exchanged phone numbers and promised to see each other again.

### Closing

It was an unexpected but pleasant experience.

### Useful Expressions

❶ While I was + V-ing
내가 ~하는 동안에
▶ While I was shopping, I saw her.

❷ Turn out
확인되다, 밝혀지다
▶ It turned out to be true.

❸ Different from...
~와 다른
▶ It was different from others.

★ 경험문제입니다. 스토리 텔링에 집중하시고 과거 시제를 능숙히 사용하는 것에 초점을 맞춰야 합니다.

## Q3. Compare your shopping habits in the past with your present ones. What are some changes? Please tell me about your shopping habits in detail.

**내용구성하기**
- **Introduction** ☑ 현재와 과거의 쇼핑 습관의 변화 소개
- **Body** ☑ 과거 쇼핑 습관  ☑ 현재 쇼핑 습관
- **Closing** ☑ 느낌 및 의견

### Introduction
Shopping has always been a favorite pastime of mine, so I go shopping frequently.

### Body
When I was younger, I used to follow trends very closely. Whenever I had some money in my pocket, I ran to the mall and spent it on whatever ❶ **caught my eye**. I often went shopping and came home with bags of clothes that I struggled to ❷ **cram into** my already packed closet.

Recently, I realized that quality is more important than quantity. Instead of looking for a bargain or a new outfit for every day of the week, I try to buy clothes that I will be able to wear and love for ❸ **years to come**. I feel that this approach makes me feel more satisfied in the long run.

### Closing
Even though I'm purchasing less now than I was before, I feel like I'm happier with the things I buy.

**Useful Expressions**

❶ Catch one's eye
시선을 끌다, 마음에 들다
▶ It caught my eyes.

❷ Cram into…
~에 쟁여놓다
▶ I crammed books into a bag.

❸ Years to come
앞으로 몇 년 간
▶ In the years to come, I hope to stay healthy.

★ 과거와 현재 비교 문제에서 과거 시제와 현재 시제의 사용에 주의해야 합니다.

**My Answer** — Use the expressions from the Key Information to develop your sentences.

— Introduction

— Body

— Closing

# OPIc 공략! IM3+

## UNIT 9
## 공연/콘서트 보기

# UNIT 09 공연/콘서트 보기

**OPIc 공략! IM3+**

## Learning Objectives
좋아하는 공연/콘서트 장르에 대해 소개하고 기억에 남는 경험 등에 대해 이야기 할 수 있다.

## Frequently Asked Questions

- What types of performances/concerts do you like to watch? Why do you enjoy them?
- Tell me what you usually do before or after going to a performance/concert.
- Tell about a memorable or recent experience going to a performance/concert.
- Have you noticed any changes in the audience when you watch a performance/concert?
- Are there any current issues or concerns in the performance/concert industry or regarding the technology used in performances/concerts?

## Brainstorming

**Step 1** Brainstorm key words and expressions about the topic.
**Step 2** Use the words and expressions to brainstorm possible questions.

### Performances and Concerts

**Place**
Q. Where do you usually go to watch a performance/concert?

**Performer/Musician**
Q. Tell me your favorite performer/musician.

**Experiences**
Q. Can you tell me about your experience?

**Activities**
Q. What do you usually do before going to a performance/concert?

## Key Information

### 콘서트/공연

Out of all the concerts/performances I have seen, I enjoyed _____ the most.
지금까지 본 콘서트/공연들 중에 _____ 가 가장 재미있었습니다.

▶ Enjoy는 동명사를 목적어로 취하는 동사이므로 동명사(-ing)형태가 목적어 자리에 온다.

The special was so impressive and innovative that I could not take my eyes off the stage.
무대의 특수 효과가 매우 인상적이고 신기해서 도저히 눈을 뗄 수가 없었습니다.

▶ So/very 형용사 that 주어 동사
이 구문에서 that절은 결과의 의미를 가지며 너무 형용사/부사 해서 주어 동사 하다 라고 해석한다.

### 뮤지션/출연자

He/She is well known for/as _____.
그/그녀는 _____ 로 유명합니다.

His/Her performances are _____.
그/그녀의 무대 공연은 _____.

I have liked him/her since _____.
_____ 때부터 그/그녀를 좋아했습니다.

▶ Since
완료 형태의 구문과 함께 쓸 때에는 ~이래로 의 뜻을 접속사로 because와 같은 ~때문에 의미를 가진다.

### 경험

I forgot to bring my ticket.
표를 갖고 가는걸 깜박했습니다.

I happened to _____ see a famous performer.
우연히 _____ 해서 유명한 공연을 보게 됐습니다.

I felt I was lucky to _____.
_____ 하게 돼서 행운이었습니다.

▶ Forget 은 동명사 to부정사 모두 목적어로 취할 수 있으며 각각이 이미하는 바가 다르니 수의해야 한다.
Forget to 부정사 to부정사 할것을 잊다. (미래)
Forget -ing ~했던 것을 잊다. (과거)

공연관람과 콘서트는 서로 유사한 질문의 형태를 가지고 있으며 콘서트도 공연의 일부분 임으로 답변의 호환성이 매우 높아 함께 학습하면 효율성을 높일 수 있습니다.

## How to Answer

**Q1.** You indicated in your survey you like to go to concerts. Tell me about what kind of concert you like to go to. Who do you go with? Why do you like to go to concerts? Tell me everything in detail.

**내용구성하기**

| | | |
|---|---|---|
| Introduction | ☑ 나의 콘서트 취향 소개 | |
| Body | ☑ 주로 가는 콘서트 종류 ☑ 함께 가는 사람 ☑ 콘서트 가는 이유 | |
| Closing | ☑ 느낌 및 의견 | |

### Introduction

I have been enjoying concerts for a long time.

### Body

I usually like to go to rock concerts and K-pop concerts. They play a lot of great songs I can enjoy and sing along to. I can experience a lively performance that you cannot see on TV. Musicians ❶ **are inclined to** invest more money in concerts to show their audience a good time and this effort is what makes a concert exhilarating.

The person I go to a concert with changes ❷ **depending on** the kind of concerts I go to. When I go to rock concerts, I always call one of my friends from high school. We loved to listen to the same rock music when we were in high school. If I want to go to a K-pop concert, I must call my cousin. She loves K-pop. She knows almost everything about K-pop and K-pop musicians. Actually, she was the one who got me into K-pop.

The major reason I love to go to concerts is probably because I feel excited when I can jump and sing along with people who share the same passion. ❸ **By doing so**, I can relieve stress.

### Closing

Anyway, each kind of concert has ❹ **something different** that I love.

### Useful Expressions

❶ Be inclined to
의향이 있다, 하고 싶어 하다
▶ I'm inclined to go to bed early.

❷ Depend on...
~에 의존하다, ~에 달려있다
▶ It would depend on the circumstances.

❸ By doing so
그렇게 함으로써
▶ There's nothing to be gained by doing so.

❹ Something different
다른 무언가
▶ She has something different.

★ 일반적 사실을 물어보는 질문으로 종류나 이유에 초점을 맞추어 대답합니다. 이런 유형의 문제는 너무 많은 정보를 답변하게 되면 다음 답변에서 중복된 정보를 줄 수 있으니 주의합니다.

# IM2 vs IM3+

| | IM2 | IM3+ |
|---|---|---|
| **Introduction** | I like to go to concerts. | I have been enjoying concerts for a long time. |
| **Body** — 주로 가는 콘서트 | My favorite kinds of concerts are rock concerts and K-pop concerts. I really like K-pop and I love Big Bang. | I usually like to go to rock concerts and K-pop concerts. They play a lot of great songs I can enjoy and sing along to. I can experience a lively performance that you cannot see on TV. Musicians are inclined to invest more money in concerts to show their audience a good time and this effort is what makes a concert exhilarating. |
| **Body** — 함께 가는 사람 | I usually go to concerts with my cousin who loves K-Pop music. | The person I go to a concert with changes depending on the kind of concerts I go to. When I go to rock concerts, I always call one of my friends from high school. We loved to listen to the same rock music when we were in high school. If I want to go to a K-pop concert, I must call my cousin. She loves K-pop. She knows almost everything about K-pop and K-pop musicians. Actually, she was the one who got me into K-pop. |
| **Body** — 콘서트 가는 이유 | When I go to concerts, I feel excited. | The major reason I love to go to concerts is probably because I feel excited when I can jump and sing along with people who share the same passion. By doing so, I can relieve stress. |
| **Closing** | That is why I like to go to concerts. | Anyway, each kind of concert has something different that I love. |

## Level Up+

IM1 IM2 ▶ IM3+

### Why IM1~IM2?

**01** My favorite kind of concert is 같은 be동사와 한국식 표현을 사용한 문장
▶ My... 가 아니라 I, 그리고 be 동사 외의 다른 일반 동사를 사용한 문장을 사용하세요.

**02** K-pop과 좋아하는 가수에 대한 정보에 초점이 맞춰있음. 이는 나중에 좋아하는 음악인 묘사 문제가 나왔을 때 반복적인 답변을 하게 만들 수 있다.
▶ 종류, 사람이나 장소에 대한 많은 정보를 주는 것이 아니라 다양한 질문에 기초정보만을 제공하세요.

**Q2.** You indicated in the survey that you enjoy watching performances. Tell me about a performance hall that you like. Where is it located? Why do you like to go there? I'd like to know what the performance hall is like inside and out.

**내용구성하기**

| | | |
|---|---|---|
| Introduction | ☑ 자주 가는 공연장 소개 | |
| Body | ☑ 공연장 이름과 위치 | ☑ 공연장 외부 묘사 |
| | ☑ 공연장 내부 묘사 | ☑ 자주 가는 이유 |
| Closing | ☑ 느낌 및 의견 | |

### Introduction

I go to performances quite often.

### Body

I love to go to the Korea Art Center. It ❶ **is located in** Seoul, which is the capital city of my country.

There are three buildings. The main performance hall is for large-scale performances. There is also a smaller performance hall, and an open theater. Between these three halls, there is a park that connects the halls. I usually go to the main hall.

The main hall is a 4-story building with a basement. In the basement, there is a coffee shop and an Italian restaurant. The food is okay but not excellent considering the high price. On the first floor, there are entrance gates and the booklets and brochures for the performances are displayed.

More seats can be found on the second and third floors. The main reason I like going there is that I can get there by any ❷ **means of transportation**. Besides, it has a big parking lot right behind the main hall, so I don't have to ❸ **worry about parking**. Above all, I love to go there because it offers the best quality performances at a reasonable price.

### Closing

It is ❹ **the perfect place for** any kind of performance.

**Useful Expressions**

❶ Be located in...
~에 위치해 있다
▶ It is located in Seoul.

❷ Means of transportation
교통수단
▶ I can get there by any means of transportation.

❸ Worry about + V-ing
~에 대해 걱정하다.
▶ Don't worry about parking.

❹ Perfect place for...
~하기에 완벽한 곳
▶ It is the perfect place for wedding.

★ 장소 묘사 문제입니다. 그림 같은 묘사는 필요하지 않습니다. "장소묘사"에서 배운 순서 (장소/이름-외부-내부-이유)로 정확한 정보전달이 중요합니다. 현재시제를 사용합니다.

**Q3.** Do you remember the first performance you watched? What was the performance about? When was it? What happened? Tell me your experience in as much detail as you can.

| 내용구성하기 | Introduction | ☑ 처음으로 봤던 공연 경험 | |
|---|---|---|---|
| | Body | ☑ 공연 관람 시기와 공연 종류 | ☑ 공연 보기 전후 상황과 공연 묘사 |
| | | ☑ 특별했던 경험 | |
| | Closing | ☑ 느낌 및 의견 | |

### Introduction

I have one very clear memory about a performance I watched.

### Body

I remember watching a magic show with my parents when I was very young. I do not remember how old I was or where it was but I can visibly remember watching some of the magic tricks.

I think it was a very special day, like someone's birthday or an anniversary. I ❶ **was dressed up** and we had a very fancy dinner before. After dinner, I went into a dark hall with heavy red curtains. A big black box was set up right in the middle of the stage. A man and women were working together. The box disappeared and a person floated in the air.

It was amazing experience for a young kid. I ❷ **was lucky** enough to be picked out among the audience. I got to participate and I got some gifts. Maybe it was my birthday.

### Closing

I did not know ❸ **what was going on at** the time but I must have been very excited to be able to vividly remember some of magic act until this day.

**Useful Expressions**

❶ Be dressed up
차려 입다
▶ I was dressed up for the party.

❷ Be enough to...
~하기에 충분한
▶ I was lucky enough to be picked.

❸ What was going on
무슨 일이었는지
▶ I didn't know what was going on since I was very little.

★ 첫번째 봤던 공연을 묘사하는 문제가 아닌 공연을 봤던 경험을 질문하는 문제입니다. 공연 차제 보다는 경험 위주의 답변을 하는 것이 좋습니다. 첫번째 경험의 기억이 없더라도 당황하지 말고 기억에 남는 경험이나 최근의 경험 등으로 대체하여 대답하여야 합니다.

**My Answer** — Use the expressions from the Key Information to develop your sentences.

— Introduction

— Body

— Closing

# OPIc 공략! IM3+

## UNIT 10

### 공원/캠핑 가기

# UNIT 10 공원/캠핑 가기

OPIc 공략! IM3+

## Learning Objectives

자주가는 공원/캠핑 장소에 대해 묘사하고 공원에서 주로 하는 활동, 캠핑 장소에서 있었던 기억에 남는 경험 등을 말할 수 있다.

## Frequently Asked Questions

- Tell me when and where you usually go. How often do you go to the park/go camping? Who do you like to go with? Why do you like to go to the park/go camping?
- Please tell me about all the activities you usually do at the park.
- Tell about a memorable or recent experience you had camping.
- Your friend wants to go to a park. Call and ask 3-4 questions about going to the park together.

## Brainstorming

**Step 1** Brainstorm key words and expressions about the topic.

**Step 2** Use the words and expressions to brainstorm possible questions.

**Park and Camping**

### Place
- Q. Tell me about a place you usually go camping.
- Q. I would like you to describe a park you like to go to.

### Things
- Q. What do you usually take when you go to the park or go camping?

### Experience
- Q. Do you have any memorable, recent, or a first experience camping?

### Activities
- Q. What do you usually do when you go to a park/go camping?

## Key Information

### 공원/캠핑장

The park I normally go to **camp in** is called _____ which is located in _____.
제가 주로 (캠핑을) 가는 공원은 _____ 인데 _____ 에 위치해 있습니다.

It was built in 1987 for the Olympics.
올림픽용으로 1987년에 만들어졌습니다.

I like it because _____.
제가 그곳을 좋아하는 이유는 _____.

▸ It is at a great location that is easily accessible by public transportation.
장소가 참 좋고 대중 교통으로 가기도 편합니다.

It offers many different facilities such as jogging tracks/hiking paths/campsites/swimming pools.
조깅트랙/하이킹코스/캠핑장/수영장 등 여러 유용한 시설을 제공하고 있습니다.

### 활동

In the park, people usually jog/hike/ride bicycles/take a walk/stroll.
공원에 온 사람들은 주로 조깅/하이킹/자전거 타기/산책을 합니다.

In-line skating/skateboarding/playing various sports/camping are common activities you can see in the park.
인라인스케이팅/스케이드보드/여러 스포츠/캠핑 활동은 공원에서 흔히 볼 수 있는 모습이죠.

People walk their dogs and play frisbee in the park.
공원에서 개를 산책시키고 프리즈비 놀이를 합니다.

▸ Take a walk와 유사단어 알아보기
Stroll : 산책하다
Wander : (목적없이) 배회하다.
Stagger : 불안정하게 비틀거리며 걷다.
Stride : 성큼성큼 걷다.

▸ 명사역할을 하는 동명사를 주어자리에 배치

▸ 복합관계부사 Whenever 주어 동사 형태
수어 동사 할 때마다 라고 해석

### 물건

Some things I usually take when I go to the park/go camping are _____.
제가 공원/캠핑을 갈 때 보통 갖고 가는 물건들은 _____ 입니다.

Whenever I go to a park/go camping I always take/bring _____.
공원/캠핑 갈 때마다 전 _____ 를 갖고/들고 갑니다.

_____ are necessary/crucial/essential items for going to the park/camping.
_____ 는 공원/캠핑을 갈 때 꼭 필요한/중요한/필수적인 물건입니다.

**Answer tips!**

공원 가기와 캠핑가기는 야외 여가활동으로 많이 선호하는 항목입니다. 이와 관련하여 공통되는 표현들을 익혀두면 보다 효율적으로 답변할 수 있습니다. 대표적인 문항유형으로는 1) 패턴(즐기는 빈도와 함께 동행하는 사람 및 장소묘사), 2) 야외활동을 즐기는 이유 및 계기(기억에 남는 경험), 3) 야외활동 할 때 챙겨가는 물건 등에 대한 질문이 있습니다. 이야기를 서술하듯 구체적으로 답변하는 연습이 필요합니다.

## How to Answer

**Q1.** You said in the survey you like to go to the park. Please tell me about activities you usually do at the park. What kind of things do you enjoy doing? Describe your perfect visit to the park from the beginning to the end.

| 내용구성하기 | | |
|---|---|---|
| Introduction | ☑ 공원 활동하기 좋은 날씨 | |
| Body | ☑ 산책하기　☑ 테니스치기　☑ 개와 함께 걷기　☑ 조깅하기 | |
| Closing | ☑ 느낌 및 의견 | |

### Introduction

These days, the weather seems to ❶ **be perfect for** people to enjoy the warm sunshine.

### Body

In the park, it is easy to see people jogging, riding bicycles, or taking a walk. I sometimes go to the park to ❷ **wander around** when I have things to think about.

Also, I frequently go to the park to use the sporting facilities available there. My favorite place in the park is the tennis courts. I usually play tennis at the park. When I am not playing tennis, I go there to ❸ **walk my dog**.

There are many people who walk their dogs at the park. I sometimes talk to them about their dogs. Recently, I have been learning to do frisbee tricks with my dog, so we dog-lovers have a lot to talk about.

When I ❹ **feel like** I need to lose weight, I go jogging or ride my bike to manage my weight.

### Closing

The activities I do vary depending on the situation but I love them all.

### Useful Expressions

❶ Be perfect for (someone) to (do something)
~에게 ~하기 완벽한
▶ It was perfect day for him to go for a ride.

❷ Wander around
돌아다니다, 헤매다
▶ I liked to wander around the park.

❸ Walk the dogs
강아지를 산책시키다
▶ I like walking the dogs in the park.

❹ Feel like...
~하고 싶다, ~한 느낌이 있다
▶ I feel like losing weight.

★ 경험을 물어보는 질문입니다. 과거시제 사용에 유의하시고 어려운 문장보다는 이야기를 시간 순서대로 서술하는 것에 초점을 맞추세요.

# IM2  IM3+

| | | IM2 | IM3+ |
|---|---|---|---|
| **Introduction** | | I often go to the park to enjoy the good weather. | These days, the weather seems to be perfect for people to enjoy the warm sunshine. |
| **Body** | 활동 1 (산책) | There are many things I can do at the park. I like to walk around the park when I have a lot to think about. | In the park, it is easy to see people jogging, riding bicycles, or taking a walk. I sometimes go to the park to wander around when I have things to think about. |
| | 활동 2 (테니스) | My favorite sports is tennis, so I like to play tennis at the tennis courts in the park. | Also, I frequently go to the park to use the sporting facilities available there. My favorite place in the park is the tennis courts. I usually play tennis at the park. When I am not playing tennis, I go there to walk my dog. |
| | 활동 3 (애완견) | There are also many people who take their dogs to the park. I like to talk to them when I go to the park with my dog. | There are many people who walk their dogs at the park. I sometimes talk to them about their dogs. Recently, I have been learning to do frisbee tricks with my dog, so we dog-lovers have a lot to talk about. |
| | 활동 4 (조깅) | | When I feel like I need to lose weight, I go jogging or ride my bike to manage my weight. |
| **Closing** | | There are many things to do at the park and I feel very happy whenever I go. | The activities I do vary depending on the situation but I love them all. |

### Level Up⁺     IM1  IM2 ▶ IM3+

**Why IM1~IM2?**

**01** "I like"와 같은 문장 반복 사용
▶ 다양한 문장 형태와 단어를 사용하여 답변을 풍성하게 만들어 보세요.

**02** 질문에 대한 직접적인 답변만 단순히 나열함
▶ 근거를 구체적으로 제시하며 질문의 테마인 공원과 연관되는 답변을 구성하세요.

**Q2.** You indicated in the survey that you like to go camping. Do you have any memorable experiences while camping? When was it? Who did you go with? What happened?

**내용구성하기**

- **Introduction** ☑ 기억에 남는 캠핑 경험 소개
- **Body** ☑ 캠핑간 시기와 장소   ☑ 캠핑 활동   ☑ 위기 상황
- **Closing** ☑ 느낌 및 의견

### Introduction

I remember one particular camping trip I went on with my family.

### Body

When I was 12 years old, my family went camping at a mountain with a narrow stream.

❶ **As soon as** we arrived at the camping site, we set up our tents and started to prepare dinner. Because we were all tired, we decided to have a simple dinner. My father had a big barbecue planned for the next day. We put our big icebox full of meat, vegetables, and fruit into the stream to protect them from ❷ **going bad** in the strong summer sunshine.

But that night, there was a heavy rainstorm and when the second day came, we realized all the food we had stored in the water was gone. Actually, that was not our biggest problem. We had set up our tents on the other side of the steam so to leave the camping site, we had to cross the water.

However, it was flooded and had a powerful current. ❸ **Any attempt to** cross the stream would require risking our lives. At that time, we did not have a cell phone. The only thing we could do was scream for help.

Fortunately, a rescue team spotted us and helped us get out of the site. I did not realize how serious it was since I was pretty young at the time. It was just a fun and exciting experience for me.

### Closing

But now I know how dangerous it was and I am thankful we got home okay.

**Useful Expressions**

❶ As soon as…
~하자 마자
▶ Please call me as soon as you can.

❷ Go bad
상하다
▶ The food went bad.

❸ Any attempt to…
~하려는 어떠한 시도
▶ She prevented me from making any attempt to escape.

★ 활동 문제는 현재시제로 답변하는 것이 최선이라는 것을 기억하세요. 본인의 활동을 설명하기엔 답변이 조금 짧아 질 수 있으니 본인이 하는 활동 이외에 일반적으로 볼 수 있는 활동들을 첨부하면 답변이 길어 질 수 있습니다.

**Q3.** Do you remember the last time you went to the park? Where did you go? When did you go? Who did you go with? What happened? Describe your last visit to the park in detail.

| 내용구성하기 | Introduction | ✓ 최근 공원에 간 경험 | | |
|---|---|---|---|---|
| | Body | ✓ 공원의 느낌 | ✓ 가지고 간 물건 | ✓ 공원에서 한 활동 |
| | Closing | ✓ 느낌 및 의견 | | |

### Introduction

I go to the park frequently and my most recent visit was last weekend.

### Body

Last Sunday I went to the park to walk around. It ❶ **had been a long time** since we had a warm day like last Sunday.

I felt like spring was right ❷ **around the corner**, so I packed a bottle of water and headed out to the park. As I expected, there were already a lot of people enjoying the warm weather. Soon I was one of them.

I unfolded my blanket and sat on it. I read a book, drank water and ❸ **took a short nap**. Everything was perfect.

In the afternoon, the wind got little stronger, so I returned home. It was pretty good.

### Closing

As soon as spring comes, I hope to enjoy many more beautiful days at the park.

**Useful Expressions**

❶ Had been a long time
오랜 시간이 흘렀다
▶ It had been a long time since I was a kid.

❷ Around the corner
목전에 있는, 아주 가까운
▶ Spring is around the corner

❸ Take a nap
낮잠을 자다
▶ Toddlers usually take naps in the afternoon.

★ 최근 경험문제 입니다. 최근 경험은 특별한 에피소드 없이 단순한 시간 순서대로의 경험을 과거시제를 사용하여 남겨주시면 됩니다.

 **My Answer** Use the expressions from the Key Information to develop your sentences.

– Introduction

– Body

– Closing

# OPIc 공략! IM3+

## UNIT 11

## 음악 감상하기

# UNIT 11 음악 감상하기

**OPIc 공략! IM3+**

## Learning Objectives

내가 좋아하는 음악 장르 및 가수, 음악을 좋아하는 이유 등에 대해 말할 수 있다.

## Frequently Asked Questions

- What type of music do you like to listen to? Why do you enjoy music?
- Tell me about the song you like to listen to the most.
- Have you had a memorable experience while listening to music?
- When did you first become interested in music? What changes have been made in the music styles that you are interested in?
- What changes have been made in the music devices and equipment you used in the past compared to now?

## Brainstorming

**Step 1** Brainstorm key words and expressions about the topic.
**Step 2** Use the words and expressions to brainstorm possible questions.

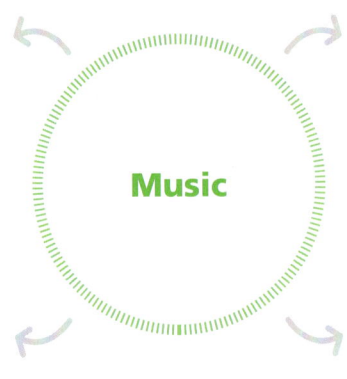

**Song**
Q. What song or music do you like to listen to the most?

**Singer/Performer**
Q. Tell me about the singer or performer you like the most.

**Gadget/Equipment**
Q. Describe a device or the equipment that you use when listening to music.

**Experience**
Q. How did you first get interested in listening to music?

# Key Information

### 음악/노래

I usually listen to _____.

제가 보통 듣는 건 _____ 이에요.

_____ is one of my favorite songs.

제가 보통 듣는 건 _____ 이에요.

It was composed/performed/sung by _____.

그 노래의 작곡자/공연자/가수는 _____ 입니다.

What I like about that song is its beautiful **lyrics/amazing melody/exciting beats/powerful performance**.

제가 그 노래를 좋아하는 이유는 가사가 아름다워서/멜로디가 멋져서/리듬이 신나서/공연이 파워풀해서입니다.

▶ 비슷한 use의 구문형태 구분
Used to 동사 동사 하곤 했다.
Be used to -ing ~하는데 익숙하다.
Be used (to 동사) (동사)하는 데 사용되다.

### 장치류

People normally use _____ to listen to music.

사람들은 음악을 듣고 싶을 때 주로 _____ 를 사용합니다.

Before it was invented, I had difficulties enjoying music anywhere and anytime.

그것이 나오기 전에는 시간 장소에 상관없이 음악을 듣기가 어려웠습니다.

**However/but/yet** thanks to the **smart-phone/mp3 player/CD player**, I can listen to what I like wherever I go and whenever I want.

그러나/하지만 스마트폰/mp3플레이어/CD 플레이어 덕분에 어디에 가든 아무 때나 좋아하는 걸 들을 수 있습니다.

### 경험

I first became familiar with music when _____.

제가 처음으로 음악과 친해진 때는 _____ 입니다.

_____ was the one who influenced me.

_____ 가 제게 영향을 줬습니다.

After graduating from **high school/college/university**, I was drawn to _____.

고등학교/대학/대학교를 졸업한 뒤에 _____ 에 마음이 끌리게 됐습니다.

▶ Graduate 은 자동사로 ~로부터 졸업하다 라는 의미로 사용할 때에는 전치사 from과 함께 쓴다.

음악감상하기는 취미나 관심사 주제 중 가장 많이 선택하는 항목 중 하나입니다. 자주 출제되는 질문 유형으로는 1) 패턴(언제, 어디에서, 즐기는 빈도), 2) 좋아하는 장르, 3) 특별히 기억에 남는 일화(관심을 갖게 된 계기, 관심의 변화 및 본인에게 끼친 영향) 등이 있습니다. 음악 관련하여 최근 자주 나오는 문제(음악을 듣기 기기)의 유형을 파악하여 미리 준비하는 것이 중요합니다. 음악의 첫번째 경험은 그 유형이 특이함으로 주의하세요.

## How to Answer

**Q1.** What changes have been made in the music gadgets and equipment that you use to listen to music? Please tell me about changes you have seen over time.

**내용구성하기**

| | |
|---|---|
| **Introduction** | ☑ 음악 기기의 변화 소개 |
| **Body** | ☑ 과거 CD와 카세트 설명   ☑ MP3파일의 도입과 MP3플레이어 |
| | ☑ 스마트폰   ☑ 카스테레오 |
| **Closing** | ☑ 느낌 및 의견 |

### Introduction

As I said, I have enjoyed music for a long time and have used several gadgets.

### Body

When I was young, I used cassette players or CD players to listen to music since that was how music ❶ **was released** at that time. Later, portable cassette players and CD players were available and they quickly became very popular around the world. But they were not really convenient due to their large size and weight.

Soon, innovation in technology changed the whole industry. Each music track could ❷ **be converted into** smaller MP3 files, which enabled people to listen to music wherever they went ❸ **as long as** they had a device to play it on. Soon MP3 players were available and everyone began using these very small devices to listen to music.

Now, smartphones and tablet pcs have become another way that people can enjoy music. The great thing about smartphones is that we do not have to carry 2 devices around anymore.

I often use my phone to play music but still, the best way for me to fully appreciate music is my car stereo. Listening to my favorite songs in the car while driving down a quiet road is something I like to do when I really want to enjoy music.

### Useful Expressions

❶ Be released
개봉되다, 출시되다
▶ New movies were released.

❷ Be converted into…
~으로 전환되다
▶ The signal will be converted into digital code.

❸ As long as…
~하는 동안에는
▶ We'll go as long as the weather is good.

### Closing

I think you should try it if you do not do this already.

★ 최근 음악 기기에 관련된 문제들이 많이 출제 되고 있으니 참고하시어 준비하시는 것이 좋습니다.

# IM2 vs IM3+

| | | IM2 | IM3+ |
|---|---|---|---|
| Introduction | | It is a very difficult question. I will tell about all gadgets I remember using. | As I said, I have enjoyed music for a long time and have used several gadgets. |
| Body | 과거 음악 플레이어 | First, there was the cassette player. It is an old gadget and was very popular. Then it was made into the smaller Walkman. | When I was young, I used cassette players or CD players to listen to music since that was how music was released at that time. Later, portable cassette players and CD players were available and they quickly became very popular around the world. But they were not really convenient due to their large size and weight. |
| | 기술의 변화 | After the Walkman, CD players came out. It was more convenient than a cassette player as it was much smaller. It was also much easier to take around. | Soon, innovation in technology changed the whole industry. Each music track could be converted into smaller MP3 files, which enabled people to listen to music wherever they went as long as they had a device to play it on. Soon MP3 players were available and everyone began using these very small devices to listen to music. |
| | 현재의 음악 플레이어 | About 10 years ago, MP3 players came out and they were really small. | Now, smartphones and tablet pcs have become another way that people can enjoy music. The great thing about smartphones is that we do not have to carry 2 devices around anymore. |
| | 내가 사용하는 음악 플레이어 | Now I use my smartphone to listen to music. | I often use my phone to play music but still, the best way for me to fully appreciate music is my car stereo. Listening to my favorite songs in the car while driving down a quiet road is something I like to do when I really want to enjoy music. |
| Closing | | They are some of the gadgets I have used. | I think you should try it if you do not do this already. |

IM1 IM2 ▶ IM3+

### Why IM1~IM2?

 어려운 문제를 대비하여 외운 듯 한 불필요한 첫

▶ 모든 문제에 대답할 수 있는 틀을 갖춘 문장이 아닌 주제와 문제에 부합한 문장을 사용합니다. 기기의 변화를 소개만 하고 왜 더 편한지 어떻게 다른 기기를 사용하게 되었는지에 대한 세부적인 이유나 설명이 없습니다.

▶ 자세하게 이유와 적절한 기기 설명을 첨가하세요.

**Q2.** You indicated in the survey that you enjoy listening to music. How often do you listen to music? When and where do you usually listen to music? What kind of music do you usually listen to? Please tell me why you listen to music. Does music affect how you feel? Tell me in as much detail as possible.

**내용구성하기**

| | | |
|---|---|---|
| **Introduction** | ☑ 음악 취향 | |
| **Body** | ☑ 좋아하는 음악 종류 | ☑ K-pop의 특징과 좋아하는 가수 |
| | ☑ 음악 듣는 시간과 장소 | ☑ 혼자 음악듣는 이유 |
| **Closing** | ☑ 느낌 및 의견 | |

### Introduction

I do enjoy listening to music.

### Body

I usually listen to various types of music. Lately, what I truly enjoy listening to is Korean Pop Music. It is getting really popular around the world as well as in my country.

It features trendy melodies and well-prepared performances. I ❶ **am proud of** Korean songs being recognized. I especially enjoy the music of Big Bang and Twice. If you listen to them, I guarantee that you will love them.

Anyway, I ❷ **tend to** listen to music while walking or driving. Unfortunately, these are the only moments I can actually focus on myself and enjoy music.

I normally listen to music alone. Frankly, I like to ❸ **be alone** when listening to music. I do not want to be disturbed.

### Closing

This is how I enjoy music. I hope this is enough.

### Useful Expressions

❶ Be proud of
자랑스러워 하다
▶ I am proud of you.

❷ Tend to
경향이 있다
▶ I tend to become emotional.

❸ Be alone
혼자 있다, 고립무원이다
▶ I like being alone.

★ 좋아하는 노래가 누구의 노래인지를 물어보는 질문이 있지만 이 문제의 핵심은 아닙니다. 노래나 가수에 대해서 너무 깊게 설명하는 것은 다음 질문에 비슷한 대답을 할 가능성이 있으니 주의하세요.

## Q3. When did you first become interested in music? Did anyone influence your musical preferences? Do you still listen to the same kind of music you did when you were a child? If not, how have your preferences changed?

**내용구성하기**

| | | |
|---|---|---|
| **Introduction** | ☑ 음악을 처음 접한 경험 | |
| **Body** | ☑ 음악을 접한 계기 | |
| | ☑ 초기의 음악 취향 | ☑ 음악 취향의 변화 |
| **Closing** | ☑ 느낌 및 의견 | |

### Introduction

I feel like music has been around me ever since I was born.

### Body

My mother is a cellist. She used to practice for her performances at home. I have been listening to my mother play her cello ❶ **as far back as I can remember**.

Therefore, I must say that my mother is the key influence for my love of music. I ❷ **was so impressed with** her passion that I could not think of anything but classical music.

Since a young age, I have not only listened to classical music but I have also learned how to play it on different musical instruments. Until the age of 15, I was only interested in classical music.

However, as I spent more time around my friends, I became interested in Korean pop. It helped me get through my high school years. Lately, I listen to music that has beautiful and touching lyrics ❸ **regardless of** its genre.

### Closing

Nowadays, I feel that I have finally come to truly appreciate and enjoy music.

**Useful Expressions**

❶ As far as I remember
내 기억으로는
▶ He was wearing short pants as far as I remember.

❷ Be impressed with...
~에 감동받다
▶ I was impressed with your message.

❸ Regardless of...
~에 상관 없이
▶ I like everyone regardless of their gender.

★ 첫번째 경험과 과거와 현재와의 변화의 문제가 통합된 형태입니다.
음악을 좋아하게 된 계기와 취향의 변화를 함께 답변으로 구성하는 것이 좋습니다.

**Use the expressions from the Key Information to develop your sentences.**

— Introduction

— Body

— Closing

# IM2 vs IM3+

| | | IM2 | IM3+ |
|---|---|---|---|
| **Introduction** | | My favorite food is Samgyetang. | I am very excited to introduce a dish that I like to cook. |
| **Body** | 요리 이름 | It is a kind of chicken soup. All chicken is in the soup. | It is called Samgyetang, a kind of chicken soup. The biggest difference between Samgyetang and chicken soup is that there is a whole chicken in the soup. |
| | 재료 설명 | The ingredients are garlic, a ginseng, Chinese dates, sticky rice, and herbs but you can change it. You add salt before eating the soup. | You do not need a lot of ingredients. Of course, you need a whole chicken. Then, a clove of garlic to eliminate any bad smell, and a piece of ginseng root. You can add more ingredients such as a couple of Chinese dates, a handful of sticky rice and various Asian herbs according to personal taste. Wait until you eat it before adding salt. You can add as much salt as you like. |
| | 좋아하는 이유 | I really like Samgyetang because cooking it is easy. Also, it is a nutritious meal. | It is a very popular dish especially in summer because it is nutritious. I like to cook Samgyetang because it is easy to make. I just add in all ingredients and boil them in a pot. If you know how to boil water, you can cook delicious Samgyetang. |
| **Closing** | | It is very easy so you must try it. | If you have not tried it yet, try to cook Samgyetang. You will love the results. |

## Level Up+

### Why IM1~IM2?

**01** '전체' 이란 뜻을 가진 문맥에는 다소 어색한 'all'을 사용해 'all chicken' 이라는 단어 조합을 사용
   ▶ 전체 이란 뜻을 가지고 문맥에 맞는 표현 **whole**을 사용하세요.

**02** 단순 열거된 재료들
   ▶ 좀 더 정확한 양과 재료를 넣는 이유를 상세히 기술하세요.

**03** 전체적으로 짧은 답변
   ▶ 재료를 넣는 이유 뿐만 아니라 좋아하는 이유를 세부적으로 말하고 만드는 방법도 간단히 넣으면서 조금 더 긴 답변을 완성하세요.

**Q2.** You indicated in the survey that you like to cook. What can you cook the best? What kind of ingredients do you usually use? Tell me about the recipe that you are the best at cooking.

| 내용구성하기 | | | | | |
|---|---|---|---|---|---|
| | **Introduction** | ☑ 요리법 소개 | | | |
| | **Body** | ☑ 요리 소개 | ☑ 면익히기 | ☑ 소스만들기 | ☑ 마무리 |
| | **Closing** | ☑ 느낌 및 의견 | | | |

### Introduction

Even though I ❶ **am not very good at cooking**, I have tried to make various dishes.

### Body

❷ **So far**, I think I can cook pasta really well. It is much more easier to make than I expected. That is the main reason I enjoy cooking pasta dishes. Also, it does not take long to prepare.

First of all, I boil water to cook the noodles. I can choose from many kinds of noodles. I love fettuccini, which is a wide noodle. Once the water boils, I put in the noodle ❸ **of my choice** and wait for about 15 minutes. When the noodles become soft, I drain the water.

In another pan, with a small amount of oil, I stir-fry minced garlic and pour in tomato sauce or heavy cream. I can add anything I want to the noodles. I usually choose shrimp, bacon, or mushrooms.

Then, I let it simmer for a few minutes before adding the noodles. After that, I just stir it three to four times, and it is done. It only takes 20 minutes to 30 minutes maximum.

### Closing

This is one simple and delicious meal I can cook.

### Useful Expressions

❶ Be good at -ing
~를 잘한다
▶ I am good at swimming.

❷ So far
지금까지
▶ So far so good

❸ ... of my choice
내가 원하는~
▶ I put in the noodle of my choice.

★ 요리하기에서 많이 나오는 요리법에 관련된 질문입니다. 요리에 관련된 기본적인 어휘를 숙지하고 답변을 준비해야 합니다.

## Q3.
When did you first become interested in cooking? Did anyone influence you? I would like to know why you started to enjoy cooking in as much detail as possible.

**내용구성하기**

| | | |
|---|---|---|
| **Introduction** | ✓ 요리에 대한 첫 느낌 | |
| **Body** | ✓ 요리를 하게된 계기 ✓ 실수했던 경험 ✓ 요리를 좋아하는 이유 | |
| **Closing** | ✓ 느낌 및 의견 | |

### Introduction
In the beginning, I did not like cooking.

### Body
I used to live with my parents and my mother is an excellent cook, so there was ❶ **no need to cook**. But when I ❷ **moved out** of my parents' house to go to university, I had to learn.

At that time, there was no one around to inspire or influence me, so it was very challenging at first. I burnt several pans and pots and did not even know how to boil an egg. They always ended up totally uncooked or burnt. After many ❸ **trials and errors**, I eventually realized how interesting it could be.

Since it has only been three years since I learned to cook, I am not very good at it but I have learned to enjoy cooking. One great thing about cooking is that I can save money and also make healthier choices.

### Closing
This is the story of how I became interested in cooking.

**Useful Expressions**

❶ No need to…
~할 필요가 없다
▶ There is no need to work.

❷ Move out of…
~에서 나오다
▶ I want to move out of my parents' house.

❸ Trials and errors
시행착오
▶ I went through many trials and errors.

★ 어떻게 음식을 만들기 시작했는지 계기를 세부적으로 기술하는 것이 답변에 핵심입니다.

**My Answer** — Use the expressions from the Key Information to develop your sentences.

- Introduction

- Body

- Closing

# OPIc 공략! IM3+

## UNIT 13
### 조깅/걷기

# UNIT 13 조깅/걷기

OPIc 공략! IM3+

## Learning Objectives

평소 조깅하는 장소를 소개하고, 조깅하기/걷기의 장점 및 주의점 등에 대해 말할 수 있다.

## Frequently Asked Questions

- I'd like to know how often and where you usually jog/walk? Why do you like to jog/walk?
- Tell me your favorite place for jogging/walking.
- What clothes or shoes do you normally wear when you go jogging/walking?
- What steps do you take to avoid slight or serious injuries while jogging/walking?
- What are some good things about jogging/walking?
- Do you have any memorable or recent experiences jogging/walking?

## Brainstorming

**Step 1** Brainstorm key words and expressions about the topic.
**Step 2** Use the words and expressions to brainstorm possible questions.

**Jogging and Walking**

**Place**
Q. Describe the place you usually go jogging/walking to me.

**Things**
Q. What do you need when you go jogging or go for a walk?

**Activities**
Q. Tell me some good things about jogging/walking.

**Experience**
Q. Do you have any experiences jogging/walking?

# Key Information

### 장소

I usually go jogging/walking at _____.
제가 조깅/산책하러 자주 가는 곳은 _____ 입니다.

_____ is where I normally go to enjoy jogging/walking.
_____ 는 제가 조깅/산책하러 가는 곳이에요.

A paved jogging/walking path is located next to the **lake/right beside the camping ground/around the park**.
고무로 포장된 조깅/산책 코스가 호수 주변을 따라/캠핑장 바로 옆에/ 공원 주변에 있습니다.

The main reason I like to go there is that **it is located close to my home/ it is quiet so I can collect my thoughts/ it has other useful facilities.**
그곳에 즐겨 가는 이유는 집에서 가까워서/조용해서 생각을 정리할 수 있어서/ 유용한 시설이 있어서 입니다.

### 장점

Jogging/walking is a good way to keep fit.
조깅/산책은 건강을 유지하는 좋은 방법입니다.

You don't have to spend a lot of money to stay in shape.
건강을 유지하느라 많은 돈을 들일 필요가 없죠.

You can exercise anywhere and any time you want.
언제 어디서나 운동을 할 수 있습니다.

You do not have to learn how to jog/walk unlike other sports.
다른 운동과 달리 조깅/산책은 따로 운동법을 배울 필요가 없죠.

### 경험

One day, I went to 장소 with _____ to _____.
하루는 (장소)로 _____ 와 _____ 하러 갔습니다.

I saw something coming toward me.
무엇인가가 내게 다가오는 것이 보였습니다.

I tripped and fell down on the ground.
발을 헛디뎌 바닥에 넘어졌습니다.

I noticed someone following me.
누군가 나를 쫓아오는 걸 알아챘습니다.

▶ Anywhere you can anytime you want 는 wherever you can and whenever you want 로 바꿔 사용할 수 있다.

▶ 의문사+to부정사 는 문장에서 명사처럼 주어, 목적어, 보어역할을 할 수 있지만 주로 목적어 역할을 한다.

▶ Fall의 과거형과 과거분사형 주의
Fall – Fell – Fallen (자동사)

### Answer tips!

운동에 관한 다양한 설문항목 중 규칙적으로 즐길 수 있는 항목을 공통으로 준비하면 효율적입니다. 운동 관련한 질문 유형으로는 1) 운동패턴(얼마나 자주, 언제, 어디에서 하는지), 2) 즐겨가는 운동장소 묘사와 그 이유, 3) 즐기는 운동에 관심을 갖게 된 계기(운동을 하는 이유) 및 기억에 남는 경험(운동하는 방법 및 절차 포함) 등에 있습니다. 관련된 어휘와 표현을 익혀 답변을 구성해보도록 합니다. 조깅하기와 걷기는 서로 다른 설문조사 항목이지만 문제의 유형과 답변의 형태가 비슷하여 함께 준비하면 좀 더 효율적으로 학습할 수 있습니다

## How to Answer

**Q1.** What are some good things about jogging compared to other sports? I'd like to know more about the advantages of jogging. Explain at least three advantages of jogging to me.

| 내용구성하기 | | |
|---|---|---|
| Introduction | ✓ 도입 | |
| Body | ✓ 특별 장비 필요 없음　✓ 배워서 할 필요 없음　✓ 장소 구속 없음 | |
| Closing | ✓ 느낌 및 의견 | |

### Introduction

I enjoy jogging whenever I can ❶ **spare some time** for it.

### Body

The greatest advantage of jogging is its accessibility. What I mean is that when people jog, they do not need to buy any special equipment. I used to play tennis but to play it, in addition to reserving a court, I needed to bring my racquet, a ball, shoes, and comfortable clothes. But for jogging, ❷ **all I need is** a pair of shoes and comfortable clothes. I do not have to buy any expensive equipment.

Moreover, there isn't any one correct way to do it. With other sports, you need to learn things like how to swing or various other skills but jogging does not take any time to learn.

You just need to find a place you would like to run. You may have to find somewhere to go jogging but if you ❸ **are willing to** jog, you can find a place to do it wherever you go.

### Closing

Jogging is the best way I've found to ❹ **keep fit** so far.

### Useful Expressions

❶ Spare time
시간을 할애하다
▶ I can spare some time for you.

❷ All I need is
내가 필요한 건 단지
▶ All I need is love.

❸ Be willing to…
기꺼이 ~ 하다
▶ He was willing to give up his seat.

❹ Keep fit
건강을 유지하다
▶ I want to keep fit.

★ 비교의 문제의 형태로 다른 스포츠와 다른점들을 언급하는 형태의 답변을 구성하는 것이 접근하기에 용의합니다.

# IM2  IM3+

|  | IM2 | IM3+ |
|---|---|---|
| Introduction | There are some differences between jogging and other sports. | I enjoy jogging whenever I can spare some time for it. |
| Body — 장점 1 (장비) | The first different thing is equipment. Jogging does not need any special things like other sports. You only really need shoes and clothes. | The greatest advantage of jogging is its accessibility. What I mean is that when people jog, they do not need to buy any special equipment. I used to play tennis but to play it, in addition to reserving a court, I needed to bring my racquet, a ball, shoes, and comfortable clothes. But for jogging, all I need is a pair of shoes and comfortable clothes. I do not have to buy any expensive equipment. |
| Body — 장점 2 (수월함) | The second different thing is the rules. There are no rules for jogging. You just need to run. | Moreover, there isn't any one correct way to do it. With other sports, you need to learn things like how to swing or various other skills but jogging does not take any time to learn. |
| Body — 장점 3 (장소) | The last different thing is the place. You do not have to go to a special place for jogging. You can jog anywhere. | You just need to find a place you would like to run. You may have to find somewhere to go jogging but if you are willing to jog, you can find a place to do it wherever you go. |
| Closing | They are many differences between jogging and other sports. | Jogging is the best way I've found to keep fit so far. |

### Why IM1~IM2?

**01** 'The first different thing' 'the last different thing' 과 같은 불필요한 'thing' 반복적인 사용
▶ difference 단어를 사용 하거나 다른 형태의 주어를 사용하세요.

**02** 비슷한 형태의 도입과 마무리 문장
▶ 서로 다른 내용과 형태의 도입과 마무리로 문장을 구성하세요.

**Q2.** You said you like walking. I'd like to know how often and when you usually walk. Where do you usually go to walk? With whom do you go? I would like to know why you like walking. Tell me about the reasons in detail.

**내용구성하기**

| | | |
|---|---|---|
| **Introduction** | ☑ 걷기에 대한 일반적 정보 소개 | |
| **Body** | ☑ 걷는 시기와 횟수 | ☑ 걷는 장소와 방법 |
| | ☑ 걷기를 좋아하는 이유 | |
| **Closing** | ☑ 느낌 및 의견 | |

### Introduction

Although I do many kinds of sports, I like walking a lot.

### Body

I normally ① **go out for a walk** almost every day before work, during lunch, and after work.

I intentionally walk to work in the morning. It takes about 20 minutes. After lunch, I walk around the office buildings while talking to my co-workers. If it is not too late after work, I walk back home. I do this because I do not have much time to exercise. I do not go to any particular place to go walking. I just choose to walk whenever I can.

② **As a matter of fact**, I really like walking. While walking, I can think about problems that are bothering me and ③ **plan things out** in advance. Walking also gives me the time to restore myself.

### Closing

That is why I enjoy walking.

### Useful Expressions

① Go out for a walk
산책 나가다
▶ Do you want to go out for a walk?

② As a matter of fact
사실은, 사실상
▶ As a matter of fact, I like you.

③ Plan out
~에 대해 계획을 세우다
▶ We have to plan things out.

★ 걷기 관련된 일반적인 사실에 대한 질문입니다. 모든 문제에 자세하게 대답할 필요는 없습니다. 일반적인 대답을 많은 정보를 주지 않고 답변을 꾸며야 합니다.

**Q3.** Do you remember the first time you walked as a hobby? How did you start walking as a hobby? Did anyone influence you? Tell me everything in as much detail as possible.

| 내용구성하기 | Introduction | ☑ 기억나는 첫 번째 걷기 경험 |
|---|---|---|
| | Body | ☑ 시기 및 장소 |
| | | ☑ 사건 및 문제 해결 |
| | Closing | ☑ 느낌 및 의견 |

### Introduction

I do not remember why I started to enjoy walking but I do have a memory of one of my first walks.

### Body

When I was around 9 years old, I had a dog, a big Golden Retriever called Fido. I used to live in the countryside and my house was located ❶ **the foot of a mountain**.

Because I did not have a lot of friends living around my house, my dog was my best friend. I used to ❷ **take him for a walk** in the afternoon and it was my favorite thing to do. This is why I think that Fido was the biggest factor in me coming to enjoy walking.

One day, I went with Fido to take a walk. Suddenly, he started to bark really hard and I could see a creature wandering in front of us. It was a wild boar. I could not move because I was so afraid. Fido ran ahead and ❸ **chased it off**. Within a second, it was gone and Fido came back to me as if he wanted to see if I was alright. I could barely understand what had just happened. I could have gotten hurt but Fido saved me. ❹ **What a smart and brave dog** he was!

### Closing

Although he is gone now, I still remember the day he saved me and whenever I go on a walk, I tend to look around more frequently.

### Useful Expressions

❶ Foot of a mountain
산자락, 산기슭
▸ I used to live at the foot of a mountain.

❷ Take a walk
산책하다
▸ I like taking a walk.

❸ Chase ... off
~를 쫓아내다
▸ I chased him off.

❹ What a/an + adj. n.
얼마나 (형용사)한 (명사)인지
▸ What a beautiful flower (it is)!

★ 첫번째 경험 문제입니다. 실제 기억할 수 없는 경험을 물어보는 경우가 있는데 바로 이 문제가 그런 경우라고 할 수 있습니다. 기억 할 수 없는 경험을 물어볼 때에는 진짜 첫번째 경험이 아니라 다른 의미에서의 첫번째 경험(예를 들어 기억할 수 있는 첫번째 경험, 혹은 혼자서 했던 첫번째 경험, 졸업하고 첫번째 경험 등등)을 이야기 하면 됩니다.

 **My Answer** — Use the expressions from the Key Information to develop your sentences.

– Introduction

– Body

– Closing

# OPIc 공략! IM3+

## UNIT 14
## 하이킹/트레킹

# UNIT 14

# 하이킹/트레킹

**OPIc 공략! IM3+**

## Learning Objectives

즐겨찾는 하이킹, 트레킹 장소에 대해 소개하고 필요한 장비 및 기억에 남는 경험 등에 대해 말할 수 있다.

## Frequently Asked Questions

- I'd like to know how often and when do you usually go hiking or trekking. Why do you like to go hiking or trekking?
- What clothes or shoes do you normally wear when you go hiking or trekking?
- Tell me about the technology and special features of clothes, shoes, or gear you use when hiking or trekking.
- Are there any environmental concerns that people may have regarding trekking or hiking?

## Brainstorming

**Step 1** Brainstorm key words and expressions about the topic.
**Step 2** Use the words and expressions to brainstorm possible questions.

### Place
Q. Describe the place you usually go hiking to me.

### Shoes and Clothes
Q. Tell me what kind of shoes and clothes you wear.

### Hiking and Trekking

### Things
Q. What do you need when you go hiking or trekking?

### Experience
Q. Do you have any experiences hiking or trekking?

# Key Information

### 신발과 옷

I like shoes with soft, cushioned bottoms.
밑창이 부드럽고 쿠션 같은 신발을 좋아합니다.

I usually wear _____.
주로 입는 옷은 _____ 이에요.

It is made of a special material that retains heat and keeps your body dry.
따뜻하면서도 건조하게 유지해주는 특수 소재로 만들어져 있습니다.

▶ Be made of vs. Be made from
Be made of :
원료의 성질이나 특징 불변
Be made from :
원료의 성질이나 특징 변화

The material breathes, so you do not have to worry about getting wet feet.
통기성이 좋아서 발에 땀이 찰까봐 걱정할 필요가 없죠.

### 물건

I need _____ when I go hiking/trekking.
하이킹/트레킹을 갈 때 필요한 건 _____ 이에요.

_____ is essential for _____.
_____ 는 _____ 에 필수적이죠.

_____ is necessary to _____.
_____ 는 _____ 하는데 필요합니다.

▶ 신발을 설명할 때에는 복수라는 것을 숙지
발의 복수형도 주의
Foot 발(단수)  Feet 발(복수)

▶ Go -ing : ~하러 가다.

### 관심사

People are saying that _____.
사람들은 _____ 라고 말합니다.

I believe/think that _____.
저는 _____ 라고 생각합니다.

_____ is a serious concern.
_____ 는 가장 심각한 문제에요.

Another issue here is _____.
여기서 또 다른 문제는 _____ 죠.

앞서 학습 했던 조깅과 걷기와 비슷한 유형들의 문제 입니다. 조깅과 걷기의 대답과 유사한 답변이 나오지 않도록 준비하는 것이 중요합니다

## How to Answer

**Q1.** You said in your survey that you like to go hiking or trekking. I'd like to know more about the place you usually go hiking or trekking. What is the name of the place? Where is it located? What can you see there? Describe the place in as much detail as possible.

| 내용구성하기 | | |
|---|---|---|
| Introduction | ☑ 하이킹 트레킹 하는 장소 소개 | |
| Body | ☑ 청계산 기본 정보 | ☑ 청계산 입구주변 묘사 |
| | ☑ 청계산 내부 묘사 | ☑ 좋아하는 이유 |
| Closing | ☑ 느낌 및 의견 | |

### Introduction

I really like to go hiking and trekking when I have time.

### Body

Among the places I have visited, I would like to tell you about Cheonggye National Park. It is a park that has a reasonably sized mountain called Cheonggye.

It is located in Seoul very close to my home. Since it is a mountain, there are many ways you can get there. My favorite route is the one with the biggest parking lot.

Once you get there, the first thing you can see are the restaurants. Some of them are very popular and many people go there before or after hiking and trekking. A small, clean stream is located when you ❶ **go up the mountain** for 30 minutes. If you continue for about an hour and a half, you can reach the summit.

❷ **As I said**, it is not too high. You can see beautiful trees and magnificent scenery when you visit the park and don't forget about the restaurants with delicious dishes.

### Closing

This is why I think it is ❸ **the best place for** hiking and trekking.

### Useful Expressions

❶ Go up…
~에 올라가다
▶ He went up the mountain.

❷ As I said
내가 말했듯이
▶ As I said, it rained.

❸ The best place for…
~하기에 가장 좋은
▶ It's the best place for hiking.

★ 자주 가는 장소 묘사입니다. 앞 유닛의 장소설명하기를 참고하면 답변을 하는데 도움이 됩니다.

# IM2  IM3+

|  | | IM2 | IM3+ |
|---|---|---|---|
| **Introduction** | | I like hiking in my free time. | I really like to go hiking and trekking when I have time. |
| **Body** | 산 이름 | I like Cheonggye National Park best. | Among the places I have visited, I would like to tell you about Cheonggye National Park. It is a park that has a reasonably sized mountain called Cheonggye. |
| | 산 위치 | It is near my home. | It is located in Seoul very close to my home. Since it is a mountain, there are many ways you can get there. My favorite route is the one with the biggest parking lot. |
| | 산 내부 묘사 | There are many famous restaurants to eat at before and after hiking. There is also a stream. It takes 90 minutes to get to the top. | Once you get there, the first thing you can see are the restaurants. Some of them are very popular and many people go there before or after hiking and trekking. A small, clean stream is located when you go up the mountain for 30 minutes. If you continue for about an hour and a half, you can reach the summit. |
| | 좋아하는 이유 | | As I said, it is not too high. You can see beautiful trees and magnificent scenery when you visit the park and don't forget about the restaurants with delicious dishes. |
| **Closing** | | This is why I like that mountain. | This is why I think it is the best place for hiking and trekking. |

IM1 IM2 ▶ IM3+

### Why IM1~IM2?

**01** 'There is/are' 반복적인 구문 사용
▶ 다양한 형태의 묘사 구문을 사용하세요.

**02** 발화량과 문장수 부족
▶ 장소에 대한 일반 정보 및 외부와 내부의 묘사 문장을 늘려서 보완하세요.

**Q2.** What kind of clothes or shoes do you normally wear when you go hiking or trekking? Why do you need to wear them? Describe the clothes and shoes you usually wear in detail.

| 내용구성하기 | | | | |
|---|---|---|---|---|
| | Introduction | ✓ 주로 입는 의상과 신발 소개 | | |
| | Body | ✓ 미끄럽지 않은 신발 | ✓ 충격 흡수 가능한 신발 | |
| | | ✓ 편안한 옷 | ✓ 선명한 색의 옷 | ✓ 따뜻한 옷 |
| | Closing | ✓ 느낌 및 의견 | | |

### Introduction

I do not need a lot when I want to go hiking or trekking. But there are things I must have to ensure my safety.

### Body

One of them is ❶ **a pair of** sturdy shoes. Shoes are important if I want to ❷ **keep myself from slipping**. I do not care about the brand of the shoes, but they should have rubber soles so that I will not slip if I step on wet or icy ground.

Also, they need some type of cushion that absorbs impact. The ground is usually uneven and the cushioned soles will help me to protect my ankles and knees.

Another important thing is finding proper clothes. My clothes for hiking and trekking are extremely comfortable. They stretch easily ❸ **in all 4 directions**.

I also try to choose very vivid colors. This is so that if I get lost people can find me quickly because of my colorful clothes.

Lastly, they can ❹ **keep my body warm** even though they are not very thick. I do not know how it works but my clothes definitely keep me warm as I enjoy hiking and trekking.

### Closing

These are the shoes and clothes I normally wear when I go hiking and trekking.

**Useful Expressions**

❶ A pair of
한 쌍의
▶ I need a pair of boots.

❷ Keep oneself from -ing
~로부터 자신을 보호하다
▶ I want to keep myself from falling.

❸ In all directions
모든 방향으로, 사방으로
▶ It stretches in all directions.

❹ Keep ... warm
~를 따뜻하게 유지하다
▶ I need to keep myself warm.

★ 신발과 의상을 설명하는 문제입니다. 너무 전문적인 내용의 답변까지는 필요 없으니 평소에 쓰는 어휘로 문장을 구성합니다.

## Q3. Do you remember anything special that happened while you were hiking or trekking? If you do, please tell me about it. Where did you go? When was it? What happened? Why was it so special? Tell me about your experience in detail.

**내용구성하기**

- **Introduction** ☑ 예상치 못했던 경험
- **Body** ☑ 시기와 장소  ☑ 하이킹길에서 본 팻말
  ☑ 사슴의 등장
- **Closing** ☑ 느낌 및 의견

### Introduction

When you go hiking or trekking, there is always a possibility that you will encounter the unexpected.

### Body

I went hiking with my family about 4 years ago. We just moved into a new neighborhood and we wanted to explore the area. All of us took a walk around the neighborhood and found a hiking path that led to a small mountain. It seemed easy and flat, so we decided to follow the path.

After hiking for about 15 minutes, we saw a sign that said "❶ **Watch out for** snakes". I could not believe that there could be snakes in the middle of a residential area. I tried to ignore it but my parents couldn't. They wanted to return home immediately.

When we ❷ **were about to** go back home, something jumped out onto the path. It was a small deer. All of us screamed but the deer ❸ **was even more scared of** us than we were of it. It turned and ran in the opposite direction. After that we went back home as fast as possible. The deer was not dangerous to us but we were still very stunned.

### Closing

I hope that you won't see any wild animals unexpectedly when you are hiking or trekking.

### Useful Expressions

❶ Watch out for…
  ~를 조심해라
  ▶ Watch out for bears.

❷ Be about to…
  막 ~하려고 할 때
  ▶ They were about to go bankrupt.

❸ Be scared of…
  ~를 무서워 하다
  ▶ You are scared of your mom.

★ 조깅하기와 걷기와 비슷한 내용으로 답변을 하지 않도록 다른 종류의 이야기로 내용을 꾸며나가는 것이 중요합니다.

 **My Answer** — Use the expressions from the Key Information to develop your sentences.

— Introduction

— Body

— Closing

# OPIc 공략! IM3+

## UNIT 15

### 국내/해외 여행

# UNIT 15

## 국내/해외 여행

**OPIc 공략! IM3+**

## Learning Objectives

기억에 남는 여행지를 소개하고 사람들이 여행을 좋아하는 이유 및 여행시 고려사항 등에 대해 이야기 할 수 있다.

## Frequently Asked Questions

- Tell me about some different cities or countries you have visited.
- Describe the place you liked the most.
- What kind of things do you usually prepare before traveling?
- What do you usually do before going on a trip?
- Do you have any memorable travel experiences?
- Do you think traveling is necessary?

## Brainstorming

**Step 1** Brainstorm key words and expressions about the topic.
**Step 2** Use the words and expressions to brainstorm possible questions.

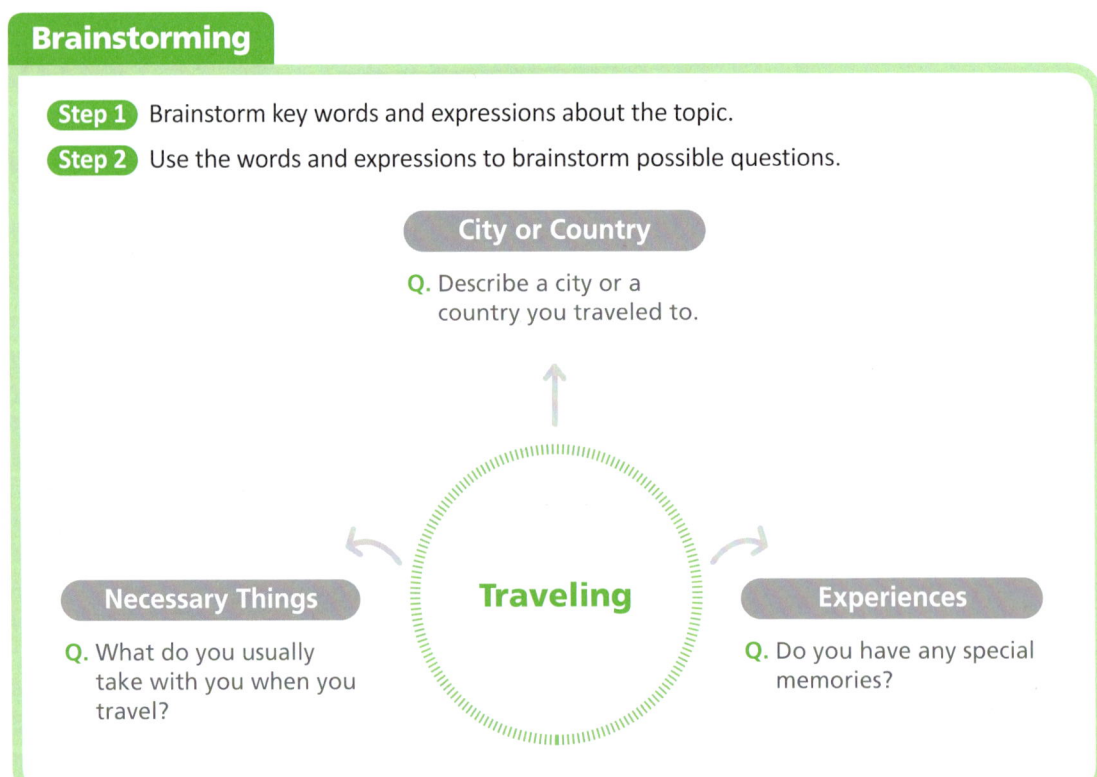

## Key Information

### 도시와 국가

So far, I have been to _____.
지금까지 _____ 에 가봤습니다.

_____ are some cities/countries that I have visited on business.
_____ 는 일 때문에 가본 도시/나라에요.

I attended a conference in _____ as well.
_____ 에서 열린 컨퍼런스에도 참석했었죠.

▶ ~에 가본적이 있다
Have gone to 장소(X)
Have been to 장소(O)

▶ As well 또한, 마찬가지로
주로 문장 뒤에 자리 한다.

### 설명

Out of all the places I have been to, I would like to talk about _____.
지금까지 가본 곳 중에서는 _____ 를 말하고 싶네요.

It is well known for _____.
그곳은 _____ 로 유명하죠.

It is most famous for _____, so a lot of people go to see it.
_____ 는 그곳의 대표적 장소로 많은 사람들이 그곳을 찾아요.

Everywhere you go, you can enjoy _____.
어딜 가든 _____ 를 즐길 수 있습니다.

▶ Be well known for... ~로 인해서
유명해지다.(이유)
Be well known as... ~(이름으)로
유명하다.

▶ Signature 는 서명이라는 뜻을 가지고
있지만 여기에서는 "상징적인/대표하는"의
의미로 사용된다.

### 사물

The first thing I do is pack my passport when I want to travel abroad.
제일 먼저 챙기는 건 해외 여행에 필요한 여권이죠.

What I need next is _____.
그 다음에 필요한 건 _____ 이에요.

It is very useful when _____.
_____ 할 때 아주 유용하죠.

Although it may not seem important to bring on a trip, I still need _____ to _____.
비록 여행에는 별로 중요해 보이지 않지만 전 그래도 _____ 하기 위해서 _____ 가 필요합니다.

국내여행과 해외여행에 관련된 질문들 입니다. 국내 여행이나 해외 여행의 질문들을 따로따로 하는 경우도 있고 city나 country로 묶어서 함께 질문하는 경우도 있습니다.

## How to Answer

**Q1.** You indicated in the survey that you like to travel. I would like to know which cities and countries you have visited. Why did you visit those places? What was the purpose of visiting those cities or countries? Tell my why you like to travel domestically or abroad.

| 내용구성하기 | | |
|---|---|---|
| Introduction | ☑ 방문한 도시와 나라들 소개 | |
| Body | ☑ 방문한 도시/나라들 | ☑ 방문 목적 |
| Closing | ☑ 여행 하는 이유 | |

### Introduction

❶ **Fortunately**, I have had many chances to travel to different cities and countries so far.

### Body

First of all, I have visited several cities in my country, Korea. I have been to Busan, Gyeongju, and Jeonju, which are all very popular travel destinations in my country. I visited them when I was in school on school field trips with my classmates and teachers. Recently, I visited Incheon to go to the biggest Chinatown in Korea.

I have also been to other countries including the U.S., Canada, France, Spain, England, Thailand, China, and so on. For the U.S. and China, I went there to ❷ **participate in** a conference as a presenter. It was a very unique experience. France and England were countries I traveled to with my friends. I visited Thailand last winter to enjoy the warm weather. It was definitely a place that I would like to visit again.

### Closing

All these traveling experiences give me the energy I need to live my daily life and also help me ❸ **relieve stress**.

### Useful Expressions

❶ Fortunately
다행스럽게도, 운 좋게도
▶ Fortunately, I won the first prize.

❷ Participate in
참가하다
▶ I wanted to participate in the contest.

❸ Relieve stress
스트레스를 풀다
▶ He needs to relieve his stress.

★ 국내 여행과 해외 여행의 문제가 통합되어 나온 구조입니다. 복수형(cities or countries) 질문이오니 한 두 군데만 세밀하게 설명하게 되면 다음 문제의 대답과 유사한 형태가 될 수 있으니 여려 도시와 나라를 세부적인 정보 없이 열거하는 것이 중요합니다.

# IM2  IM3+

|  | IM2 | IM3+ |
|---|---|---|
| **Introduction** | I like traveling and I am going to tell you about different cities and countries I went to. | Fortunately, I have had many chances to travel to different cities and countries so far. |
| **Body** — 방문한 곳 | I went to many places such as France, Italy, Spain, Thailand, and the Philippines. And I went to many Korean cities like Incheon, Sokcho, Jeonju, and Busan. | First of all, I have visited several cities in my country, Korea. I have been to Busan, Gyeongju, and Jeonju, which are all very popular travel destinations in my country. I visited them when I was in school on school field trips with my classmates and teachers. Recently, I visited Incheon to go to the biggest Chinatown in Korea. |
| **Body** — 방문 목적 | I visited Busan last winter. There was a big fireworks festival and I saw many people and ate good food. I really enjoyed the city. Also, I want to talk about my trip to Thailand. I went there for my summer vacation. Everything was perfect. I hope I can visit Thailand again. | I have also been to other countries including the U.S., Canada, France, Spain, England, Thailand, China, and so on. For the U.S. and China, I went there to participate in a conference as a presenter. It was a very unique experience. France and England were countries I traveled to with my friends. I visited Thailand last winter to enjoy the warm weather. It was definitely a place that I would like to visit again. |
| **Closing** | These are the cities and countries I have visited. | All these traveling experiences give me energy to live my daily life and also help me relieve stress. |

IM1　IM2　▶　**IM3+**

### Why IM1~IM2?

**01** 여러 도시와 나라가 아닌 한두 개의 장소에 집중된 설명과 개인 경험이 포함된 답변. 다음 질문에 반복적인 답변을 할 가능성 높음
  ▶ 한두 장소에 집중되지 않은 여러 장소에 대한 간략한 설명으로 답변을 대체하세요.

**02** 'And'와 'Also'와 같은 불필요한 접속사의 남용.
  ▶ 접속사를 최소화 하고 사용한다면 다양한 접속사를 사용하세요.

**Q2.** Among the places you have visited, choose one place that you like the most. What is the name of the place? Where is it located? What can you see there? Why do you like that place the most? Describe the place you like the most in detail.

**내용구성하기**

**Introduction** ☑ 인상깊었던 여행 장소
**Body** ☑ 전주 도시 정보  ☑ 전주 관광지 묘사
☑ 전주에서 인상 깊었던 점  ☑ 전주를 좋아하는 이유
**Closing** ☑ 느낌 및 의견

### Introduction

Of all the cities I have visited, I think Jeonju was my favorite.

### Body

Jeonju is located in the southern part of the Korean peninsula and it ❶ **is famous for its** delicious food as well as its well-preserved traditional houses.

When you enter the city from the highway, you can see a glamorous gate designed ❷ **based on** the Korean traditional house, Hanok. Once you are in the city, people tend to go to the village of traditional houses, Hanok Village, where Korean traditional houses are located.

The amazing thing about the city is that you feel ❸ **as if** you are in the middle of an old city but at the same time you do not feel uncomfortable. The streets are narrow but the police control the amount of traffic, so they are clean and pleasant. People seem to be nice and try to help tourists as much as possible.

The primary reason I visited the city was its food. Everywhere I went, I ❹ **was able to** enjoy delicious and satisfying food.

### Closing

I would like to visit this city again ❺ **if I have the chance**.

### Useful Expressions

❶ Be famous for...
~로 유명한
▶ It is famous for its food.

❷ Based on...
~에 기반을 둔
▶ The book is based on true story.

❸ As if...
마치 ~인 듯이
▶ I felt as if I was in a dream.

❹ Be able to...
~할 수 있다
▶ I was able to walk along the beach.

❺ If I have the chance
기회가 된다면
▶ If I have the chance, I want to visit there again.

★ 국내 여행과 해외 여행의 문제가 통합되어 나온 구조입니다. 앞의 문제와 비슷한 문제인 것 처럼 보이지만 사실 이 문제는 한곳을 세부적으로 묘사하는 문제입니다. 한 두곳에 집중된 대답을 하는 것이 중요합니다.

**Q3.** Tell me about the things you prepare before you go on a trip. What do you take and why do you take it? What is in your luggage? Describe the things you take in as much detail as possible.

| 내용구성하기 | | |
|---|---|---|
| | **Introduction** | ✓ 여행할 때 준비하는 물건들 |
| | **Body** | ✓ 햇빛 보호용품  ✓ 현금과 신용카드 |
| | | ✓ 스마트폰 |
| | **Closing** | ✓ 느낌 및 의견 |

### Introduction

Packing the bags is the most enjoyable part of my trip.

### Body

Regardless of the place and how many days I will be traveling, I always pack my sunscreen and sunglasses. I have very sensitive skin and eyes. If they ❶ **are exposed to** the sun for too long, they turn red quickly and become painful.

The next thing I put in my bag is cash and a credit card. Traveling without enough money makes me nervous. I want to be sure I have enough money for unexpected souvenirs or any delays. ❷ **Just in case** the unexpected happens, I always take extra cash and a credit card.

❸ **Not to mention**, I think my phone is the most important thing to pack. Without it, I cannot function at all. I need it to listen to music, for maps, to use the internet, and to call my loved ones while traveling.

I also take my ID with me whenever I go on a trip. If I go abroad, I need my passport. When I travel domestically, I always take my drivers' license and national ID card.

### Closing

These are the general things I take on my trip. Thinking about these items, it makes me want to travel somewhere right now.

**Useful Expressions**

❶ Be exposed to...
~에 노출되다
▶ I don't want to be exposed to the media.

❷ Just in case
만약, ~한 경우에 한해서
▶ Just in case I cannot make it, you can go ahead.

❸ Not to mention...
~은 말할 나위도 없고
▶ Not to mention my time and effort will be wasted.

★ 콤보 문제의 3번재 문제는 주로 경험 문제이지만 여행 경험은 쉽게 답변 할 수 있는 문제임으로 조금 생소한 물건 묘사 문제를 연습하려 합니다. 물건과 물건을 사용하는 목적 순으로 열거하고, 현재시제를 사용하는 것이 특징입니다.

 **My Answer** — Use the expressions from the Key Information to develop your sentences.

— Introduction

— Body

— Closing

# OPIc 공략! IM3+

## UNIT 16
### 집에서 휴가 보내기

# UNIT 16 집에서 휴가 보내기

OPIc 공략! IM3+

## Learning Objectives

집에서 휴가를 보내는 이유에 대해 설명하고 집에서 하는 활동, 기억에 남는 경험 들을 이야기 할 수 있다.

## Frequently Asked Questions

- Tell me about why you like to stay at home.
- What do you usually do when you spend your vacation at home?
- Do you have any memorable experiences vacationing at home?
- Tell me about a recent or your first experience vacationing at home.
- Has the way you spend a vacation at home changed over time?
- Do you believe it is necessary to have a vacation?

## Brainstorming

**Step 1** Brainstorm key words and expressions about the topic.
**Step 2** Use the words and expressions to brainstorm possible questions.

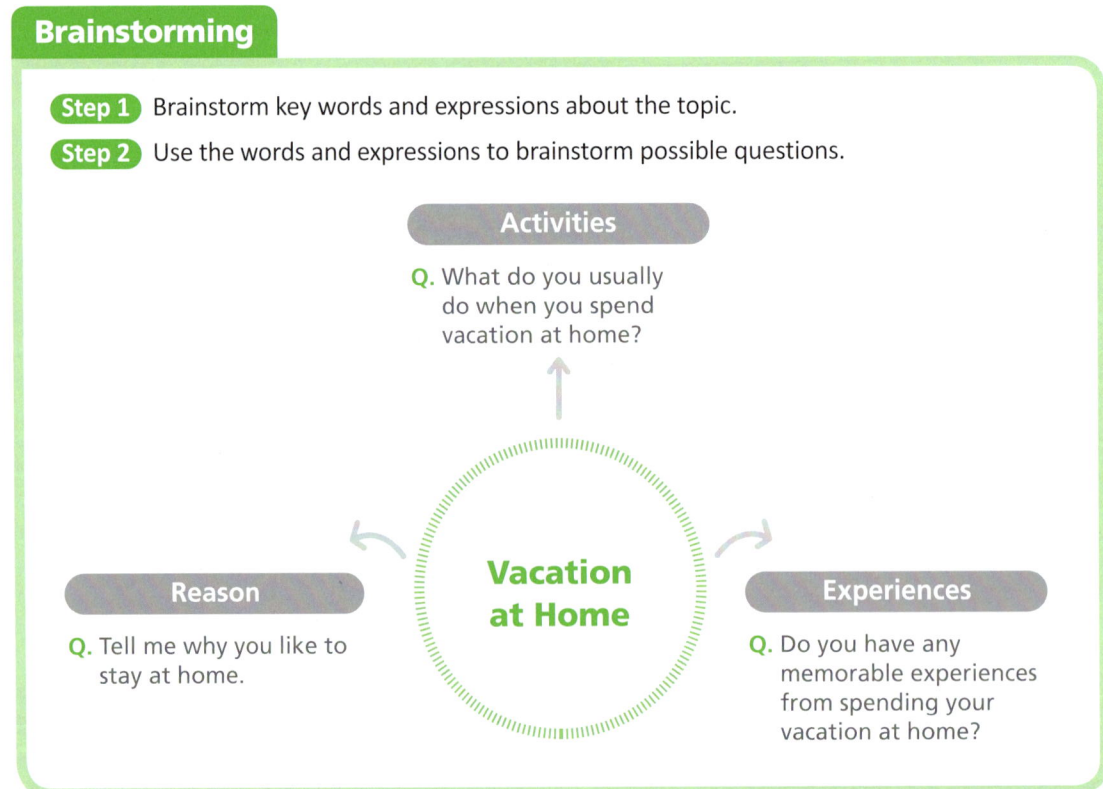

**Activities**
Q. What do you usually do when you spend vacation at home?

**Vacation at Home**

**Reason**
Q. Tell me why you like to stay at home.

**Experiences**
Q. Do you have any memorable experiences from spending your vacation at home?

# Key Information

### 이유

There are several reasons why I like to stay home.
집에 있는 것이 좋은 이유가 몇 개 있습니다.

I am so 형용사 that I cannot _____.
전 너무 _____ 해서 _____ 를 하지 못합니다.

Traffic makes me tired.
여행 목적지에 도착할 때까지 교통 체증에 갇혀있는 건 피곤한 일입니다.

My community center offers _____.
동네 주민센터에서 _____ 를 제공하고 있습니다.

▶ Why는 관계부사로 the reason을 선행사로 받고 관계부사 뒤에는 완벽한 문장이 따르게 된다. 선행사 the reason이나 관계부사 why 중 하나는 생략할 수 있다.

### 활동

I am fond of hanging out with my friends.
친구들과 어울리는 걸 정말 좋아합니다.

It is a great chance to get some time for myself.
혼자 있는 시간을 갖기에 참 좋은 기회죠.

It is natural to _____ while staying at home.
집에 있는 동안 _____ 하는 건 당연하죠.

▶ Be fond of... ~하는 것을 좋아하다.
Of는 전치사이므로 목적어는 명사형태이거나 동명사 형태이어야만 한다.

▶ For oneself 혼자서 홀로
By oneself 혼자 힘으로, 스스로

### 변화

There are several changes I have noticed when it comes to taking trips.
여행에 관해서 몇 가지 변화가 생겼습니다.

People used to _____ when traveling.
여행할 때 사람들은 _____ 하곤 하죠.

We no longer _____.
우리는 더 이상 _____ 하지 않아요.

집에서 보내는 휴가의 대표적인 질문 유형으로는 1) 집에서 휴가를 보내는 이유 2) 집에서 휴가를 보낼 때 하는 활동, 3) 집에서 휴가를 보낸 경험에 관한 것입니다. 집에서 휴가를 보내는 목적 및 활동, 함께 보내는 사람 및 관련 경험 등 기본적인 사항에 대한 어휘와 표현을 익혀 답변을 미리 준비하도록 합니다. 집에서 보내는 휴가 항목을 선택하지 않아도 돌발 질문처럼 간혹 나오는 주제이니 미리 학습을 하는 것이 좋습니다.

## How to Answer

**Q1.** I would like to know what you usually do when you spend time at home. What are some activities that you usually do during your vacation? Please answer in as much detail as you can.

| 내용구성하기 | | |
|---|---|---|
| Introduction | ✓ 집에서 휴가를 보낼 때 하는 일 | |
| Body | ✓ 잠자거나 휴식  ✓ 다양한 프로그램 참석  ✓ 친구들과 만남 | |
| Closing | ✓ 느낌 및 의견 | |

### Introduction

I ❶ **prefer to** stay at home and enjoy my free time when I am on vacation.

### Body

There are several things I can do at home. First of all, I enjoy sleeping. This is my favorite activity. I work hard and usually ❷ **stay up late** and get up early during the week, so I suffer from a constant lack of sleep. When I am on vacation or have a day off, I usually sleep a lot. I think rest is necessary for me to continue living the life I have right now.

Another activity I usually enjoy during vacation is participating in activities offered by my community center. As I said, the community center in my neighborhood offers various programs. I am planning on joining a cooking class and a tennis club this year.

In addition, when I stay at home during my vacation, I usually ❸ **meet up with** my friends. Ever since I started working, I barely have time for them. They are also in a similar situation, so it is natural for us to want to see each other when we have vacation.

### Closing

There may be a lot of things you can do on vacation but I ❹ **am very satisfied with** my vacation choices.

### Useful Expressions

❶ Prefer to…
~를 선호하다
▶ I prefer to stay at home.

❷ Stay up late
늦게까지 안자다
▶ I stayed up very late.

❸ Meet up with
만나다
▶ I met up with the friends from

❹ Be satisfied with…
~에 만족하다
▶ I was satisfied with the result.

★ 일상적인 이야기를 서술하는 것이 바람직합니다. 현재 시제 사용에 주의하세요.

# IM2  IM3+

|  | IM2 | IM3+ |
|---|---|---|
| **Introduction** | I usually stay at home when I have a vacation time. | I prefer to stay at home and enjoy my free time when I am on vacation. |
| **Body** — 휴식 | I do not do anything special. I usually sleep a lot. It is nothing exciting but I really like it. Vacation time is only time I can sleep a lot and relax. | There are several things I can do at home. First of all, I enjoy sleeping. This is my favorite activity. I work hard and usually stay up late and get up early during the week, so I suffer from a constant lack of sleep. When I am on vacation or have a day off, I usually sleep a lot. I think rest is necessary for me to continue living the life I have right now. |
| **Body** — 프로그램 참석 | Also, I like to participate in different activities. There is a community center near my house and it has many programs. I sometimes go to the center and participate in some of the programs. | Another activity I usually enjoy during vacation is participating in activities offered by my community center. As I said, the community center in my neighborhood offers various programs. I am planning on joining a cooking class and a tennis club this year. |
| **Body** — 만남 | Sometimes I meet my friends. That is what I do when I have a vacation at home. | In addition, when I stay at home during my vacation, I usually meet up with my friends. Ever since I started working, I barely have time for them. They are also in a similar situation, so it is natural for us to want to see each other when we have vacation. |
| **Closing** | My vacation is nothing special but I enjoy it. | There may be a lot of things you can do on vacation but I am very satisfied with my vacation choices. |

## Level Up⁺

IM1　IM2　▶　**IM3+**

### Why IM1~IM2?

**01** 'Vacation time'과 같이 불필요하게 사용되는 단어 'time', 'season', 'situation'등을 명사 뒤에 붙이는 한국식 표현
　▶ 올바른 표현으로 정정하세요.

**02** 짧은 단답형의 활동소개
　▶ 활동을 하는 이유와 활동에 세부적인 사항들을 추가하여 답변을 풍성하게 만들어 보세요.

**Q2.** You said in your survey that you like staying at home during vacation. Tell me why you like to stay at home.

### 내용구성하기

| | | |
|---|---|---|
| Introduction | ☑ 집에서 보내는 휴가 이유 | |
| Body | ☑ 시간이 없음 | ☑ 차량 정체나 혼잡한 장소 꺼려함 |
| | ☑ 시민회관에서 다양한 프로그램 제공 | |
| Closing | ☑ 느낌 및 의견 | |

### Introduction

I like to stay at home during my vacation.

### Body

The primary reason for me trying to stay at home is that I do not have enough time. I work almost every day and do not have ❶ **enough time to** travel or go anywhere for a long time. Even if I have a few ❷ **days off** for vacation, I want to stay at home and relax.

Another reason for me to stay at home is that I am ❸ **sick and tired of** traffic jams and crowded airports. Roads ❹ **are packed with** cars and there are too many people at the airport during the peak vacation season. I do not want to waste my precious time on the road or waiting for a delayed flight.

The last reason is that my community center offers great alternative programs. There are various activities such as tennis, painting, cycling, swimming, and art classes you can participate in.

### Closing

If you feel the same way, it is ❺ **time to** try enjoying a vacation at home.

### Useful Expressions

❶ Enough time to…
~하기 충분한 시간
▶ She had enough time to finish

❷ Day off
쉬는 날
▶ I had a day off yesterday.

❸ Sick and tired of…
~에 진절머리가 나다
▶ They were sick and tired of air pollution.

❹ Be packed with…
~로 가득 찬
▶ The bus was packed with people.

❺ Time to…
~할 시간
▶ It is time to have breakfast.

★ 이유들을 상세히 서술하는 형태의 답변이 필요합니다.

## Q3. Do you have any unforgettable memories from when you spent your vacation at home? Let me know about a special event from your vacation at home.

**내용구성하기**

- Introduction ☑ 집에서 보내는 특별한 휴가 소개
- Body ☑ 혼자 휴가 보낸 이유와 예상 밖의 즐거움 ☑ 음식과 돈이 모자람
  ☑ 언니의 음식 주문
- Closing ☑ 느낌 및 의견

### Introduction

Four or five years ago, I had to stay at home during my summer vacation.

### Body

It was not what I ❶ **had in mind**. My family and I were supposed to go on vacation together but because of my school schedule, I was not able to join them and I had to stay at home alone. I was a little disappointed but at the same time, I was glad to have some time by myself. It ❷ **turned out to** be even better than I expected. I read, watched whatever I wanted on TV, hung out with my friends and slept a lot.

One thing I did not enjoy was the food. My mom had prepared some food for me before she left but 2 days before they came back, the food ❸ **ran out**. ❹ **To make things worse**, I did not have enough money to buy more food. I spent it all, so I had to send a message to my big sister who was traveling with my parents begging for help.

Then, a great thing happened on the last 2 days. All kinds of delivery food like Chinese food, pizza, fried chicken, and noodles were delivered to me. My sister had ordered them for me with her smart phone. How amazing the world is! With her help, I was able to enjoy the end of my vacation at home.

### Closing

It was the best vacation ever!

### Useful Expressions

❶ Have ... in mind
~를 염두에 두다
▶ It was not what I had in mind.

❷ Turn out to be...
~로 밝혀지다
▶ It turned out to be even better than I expected.

❸ Run out
다 떨어지다
▶ I ran out of money.

❹ To make things worse
설상가상으로
▶ To make things worse, it rained.

 **My Answer** — Use the expressions from the Key Information to develop your sentences.

- Introduction

- Body

- Closing

# 실력다지기

☑ **Part 3  롤플레이**

**Unit 17** | EVA에게 질문하기
**Unit 18** | 전화해서 질문하기
**Unit 19** | 대안 제시하기
**Unit 20** | 상황 설명하기

# OPIc
## 공략!
## IM3+

# OPIc 공략! IM3+

## UNIT 17
### EVA에게 질문하기

# UNIT 17

## EVA에게 질문하기

OPIc 공략! IM3+

## Learning Objectives

상황과 주제를 이해하고 질문을 통해 면접관의 기호, 하는 일 및 활동 등 질문의 목적을 달성 할 수 있는 답변을 할 수 있다.

## Frequently Asked Questions

- I live with my family. Please ask me 3 or 4 questions about my family.

- I like watching movies, too. Ask me several questions about my favorite movie.

- I also like to listen to music. Ask me 2 or 3 questions to find out about my favorite genre of music.

- I like to go jogging, too. Ask me some questions to find out where I usually go jogging.

- I also like to travel to different cities and countries. Ask me several questions about it.

- I also like to go to the park. Ask me several questions to learn about the park I usually go to.

- I went shopping with my sister last weekend. Ask me 3 or 4 questions about our shopping trip.

- I also like to spend my vacation at home. Ask me a couple of questions to know about what I do to enjoy my vacation at home.

- Suppose that you're going to open a bank account. Ask a few questions to find out more about opening an account.

- You want to buy two tickets for a concert. Ask the ticket counter employee 3 or 4 questions.

- I took a training program at my company. Please ask me 3 or 4 questions about the program.

직접 질문하는 롤플레이 유형은 주어진 상황에서 질문의 주제에 대해 3~4가지 관련 질문을 하는 것입니다. 제3자 또는 질문자 에바에게 질문하는 두 가지의 유형으로 나뉩니다. 직접질문하기는 주어진 상황에 대한 질문을 얼마나 적절하고 풍부하게 구성할 수 있는지가 중요합니다. 보다 효율적으로 대비하기 위해서는 주제별(일상생활, 회사관련, 여가시간 등) 질문유형들에 익숙해지고 의문사 활용을 통해 다양한 질문들을 만들어내는 연습을 하도록 합니다.

# Key Information

### 공감과 반응

**I am glad/excited/amazed to know you like to 주제.**
당신이 주제를 좋아하는걸 알게 돼서 기쁩니다/신이 납니다/놀랍습니다.

**I did not realize you like to 주제.**
당신이 주제를 좋아하는 줄 몰랐습니다.

**I am happy to find a person who shares the same interests as me.**
나와 같은 관심사를 가진 사람을 만나서 기쁘네요.

### 종류/타입

**What kind/type of 주제 do you like?**
어떤 종류/유형의 주제를 좋아하나요?

### 시간

**When do you normally 주제?**
언제 주로 주제하십니까?

**How often do you 주제?**
얼마나 자주 주제를 하십니까?

▶ 질문할 때 제일 중요한 것은 어순이다. 의문문을 만들 때 주어 동사의 도치라는 것을 기억하자.
(의문사)+Be동사+주어~?
(의문사)+Do(es)/Did+주어+일반동사~?
(의문사)+조동사+주어+일반동사~?

### 사람

**With whom do you like to 주제?**
누구와 같이 주제를 합니까?

### 장소

**Where do you usually go to 주제?**
주제를 하러 주로 어디로 가나요?

**What can you see there?**
거기에선 뭘 볼 수 있나요?

### 선호/비선호

**What is your favorite 주제?**
가장 좋아하는 주제가 뭔가요?

**Who is your favorite 인물/사람?**
가장 좋아하는 인물/사람이 누군가요?

**Why do you like 사물/사람?**
사물/사람을 좋아하는 이유가 뭔가요?

**What does 사람 look like?**
사람은 어떻게 생겼나요?

**Do you have any _____ you do not like?**
싫어하는 _____ 이 있나요?

▶ ~해본적 있습니까? 라고 질문 할 경우에는 현재완료 시제를 사용하는 것이 적절하다.
**Have you ever (과거분사)?**

▶ **Why don't we** 는 왜 ~하지 않아?라고 묻는 것이 아니라 ~하는 것이 어때? 라는 제안의 의미를 가지는 표현이다.

앞서 이미 공부했던 묘사, 경험, 비교 등의 문제들을 그대로 다시 사용함으로써 질문하기 문제를 위한 답변을 따로 준비하지 않고도 효과적으로 대답할 수 있습니다.

## How to Answer

**Q1.** I like watching movies, too. Ask me 2 or 3 questions to find out about my favorite genre of movie, and how I choose and watch movies.

**내용구성하기**

| | | |
|---|---|---|
| Introduction | ☑ | 영화 보는 여가 활동에 공감 |
| Body | ☑ | 좋아하거나 싫어하는 영화 종류 질문 |
| | ☑ | 선호하는 영화배우와 영화 관련 질문 |
| Closing | ☑ | 의견이나 요청 |

### Introduction

I did not realize you like to watch movies. That is interesting. I would like to ask you several questions about it ❶ **if it is okay with you.**

### Body

I want to know which types of movies you enjoy. What kinds of movie do you like to watch? Are there any types of movies that you hate to watch as well? If there are, tell me what they are and why you hate them.

Could you tell me some actors and actresses you like? Why are they attractive to you? ❷ **Have you** watched their movies? Would you like to recommend any movie to me?

### Closing

That is all I wanted to ask. If it is all right with you, I hope we can ❸ **get together** some time to watch a movie.

### Useful Expressions

❶ If it is okay with you
괜찮으시다면
▶ I would like to ask a question if it's okay with you.

❷ Have + p.p.
~해본 적이 있다
▶ I have watched the movie.

❸ Get together
만나다
▶ We should get together sometime.

# IM2  IM3+

|  | | IM2 | IM3+ |
|---|---|---|---|
| **Introduction** | | I am going to ask you some questions. | I did not realize you like to watch movies. That is interesting. I would like to ask you several questions about it if it is okay with you. |
| **Body** | 좋아하는 영화 | What kinds of movies do you like? | I want to know which types of movies you enjoy. What kinds of movie do you like to watch? Are there any types of movies that you hate to watch as well? If there are, tell me what they are and why you hate them. |
| | 좋아하는 배우 | Who is your favorite actor or actress? What is your favorite movie? | Could you tell me some actors and actresses you like? Why are they attractive to you? Have you watched their movies? Would you like to recommend any movie to me? |
| **Closing** | | That is all. Thank you. | That is all I wanted to ask. If it is all right with you, I hope we can get together some time to watch a movie. |

IM1 IM2 ▶ IM3+

### Why IM1~IM2?

**01** Be동사를 주로 사용한 단순하고 반복적인 형태의 질문들
   ▶ 다양한 의문사와 동사를 사용한 서로 다른 형태의 질문들을 사용하세요.

**02** 짧은 답변
   ▶ 한 주제에 관련된 질문을 여러 개 함으로써 문장의 수와 답변의 길이를 늘려보세요.

www.carrotenglish.com 157

**Q2.** I also like to listen to music. Ask me 2 or 3 questions to find out more about my taste in music.

**내용구성하기**

| | | |
|---|---|---|
| **Introduction** | ☑ 음악 듣기 취미에 공감 | |
| **Body** | ☑ 음악 종류관련 일반 질문들 | ☑ 좋아하는 노래와 가수 관련 질문들 |
| | ☑ 경험 질문 | |
| **Closing** | ☑ 의견이나 요청 | |

### Introduction

Music is an important part of my life and I am very excited to learn that you like to listen to music, too.

### Body

First of all, what type of music do you like? Hip-hop or K-pop? ❶ **Have you ever listened to K-pop**? When do you usually listen to music? Do you have anyone you like to listen to music with? Who is that person?

What is your favorite song? Why do you ❷ **like it the most**? Who is your favorite musician? What does she or he look like? Are there any special reasons you like that person?

And lastly, have you ever met that person?

### Closing

I think listening to music ❸ **is a nice way to** relieve stress. You may think so too. I really hope to talk to you again about music we like later.

**Useful Expressions**

❶ Have you ever + p.p
   ~해본 적 있니?
   ▶ Have you ever been there?

❷ Like it the most
   가장 좋아하다
   ▶ Why do you like it the most?

❸ Is a nice way to...
   ~하기 좋은 방법이다
   ▶ Jogging is a nice way to do some light exercise.

★ 이유들을 상세히 서술하는 형태의 답변이 필요합니다.

**Q3.** I also like to travel to different cities and countries. Ask me several questions about it.

| 내용구성하기 | Introduction | ☑ 여행에 대한 공감 |
|---|---|---|
| | Body | ☑ 방문 한 도시들 묘사 질문 |
| | | ☑ 경험 질문 |
| | Closing | ☑ 의견이나 요청 |

### Introduction

I **❶ am happy to** meet someone who shares the same interest as me.

### Body

Where have you visited? Would you tell me some of the cities and countries you have been to? Tell me about a city you want to visit again. What is the name of the place? Where is it located? What does it ❷ **look like**? Why do you like that place so much?

Tell about a memorable trip you went on. Where did you go? What was so memorable to you? On the other hand, have ever had an unpleasant or unexpected experience while you were on vacation? What happened?

### Closing

There are so many questions I want to ask but ❸ **that is all for now**. I am very glad to know you like to travel just like me.

### Useful Expressions

❶ Be happy to…
~해서 기쁘다
▶ I'm happy to be here.

❷ Look like…
~처럼 보인다
▶ She looks like you.

❸ That's all for now.
지금은 그게 다예요.
▶ That's all for now. You can go.

**My Answer** — Use the expressions from the Key Information to develop your sentences.

- Introduction

- Body

- Closing

# OPIc 공략! IM3+

## UNIT 18
## 전화해서 질문하기

# UNIT 18 전화해서 질문하기

OPIc 공략! IM3+

## Learning Objectives

주어진 문제나 상황에 따라 문제 해결 및 정보 얻기 등의 특정 목적을 가지고 유선상으로 적절한 질문을 할 수 있다.

## Frequently Asked Questions

- I am going to give you a situation to act it out. You want to buy some shoes. Call the store and ask 3 or 4 questions about them.

- You have been invited to a party or community event. Call your friend and ask 3 or 4 questions about a party or event you are invited to.

- You are going on a trip to a place you have never been to. But one of your friend lives there. Call your friend and ask 3 or 4 questions about the place you are going.

- You plan to travel with your family and need to reserve a hotel room. Call a hotel and ask 3 or 4 questions to reserve a room.

- You need to finish your home improvement project by the end of the day. But you realized you have a missing part. Call the hardware store and ask 3 or 4 questions about the missing part.

- I'd like to give you a situation and ask you to act it out. You're going to take a trip and you have to rent a car. Call a rental agency and ask 3 or 4 questions about renting a car.

- I'd like to give you a situation and ask you to act it out. Let's say that a gym has just opened in your neighborhood. Call the gym and ask 3 or 4 questions about it.

전화로 질문하기 유형은 상대방에게 직접 질문하는 것과 달리 전화통화하는 상황이 추가된 것입니다. 따라서 전화통화하는 상황에서 사용할 수 있는 표현들과 전화 대화형식(인사말→전화용건→질문하기→끝인사)을 익혀두는 것이 중요합니다. 각 주제별 출제될 수 있는 질문유형을 이해하고 전화를 받게 될 대상과 주제에 따라 전화 통화 형식의 답변을 준비하도록 합니다.

## Key Information

### 전화표현

Hello, this is 이름 calling.
안녕하세요, 전 이름 입니다.

▶ 전화 통화에서 "나"는 this로 지칭한다.

### 상황/이유 설명

I called you to ask several questions about _____.
_____에 관해 몇 가지 여쭤보려고 전화 드렸습니다.

Can you help me to _____?
_____하는 걸 좀 도와주시겠어요?

▶ Help는 준사역 동사로 목적어와 목적격 보어를 수반하는데 목적격 보어 자리에 to 부정사나 동사 원형을 사용할 수 있다.

I would like to ask some questions to learn more about _____.
_____에 대해 알고자 몇 가지 질문을 드리고 싶습니다.

Do you mind if I ask a few questions about _____?
_____에 대해 몇 가지 질문을 드려도 괜찮을까요?

▶ Mind
~를 꺼려하다 라는 의미.
*목적어 자리에 if절 혹은 동명사구를 사용할 수도 있다.
Do you mind -ing?

### 상품이나 물건

How much does it cost?
이건 얼마인가요?

What are some special features?
특수 기능이 무엇인가요?

Do you have it in any other colors?
이 제품으로 다른 색상이 있나요?

Do you offer any discounts?
할인이 가능한가요?

### 초대

Where is the party/event going to be held?
파티/이벤트는 어디서 열립니까?

When will the party/event take place?
파티/이벤트는 언제 열리나요?

Is it okay for me to be late?
늦게 가도 괜찮을까요?

Do I need to prepare anything for the party/event?
파티/이벤트를 위해 준비해야 할 게 있나요?

바로 질문에 답변하는 것 보다는 주어진 상황과 질문 하는 이유를 상세히 설명하는 것이 필요합니다. 3-4개의 질문에 너무 집착할 필요 없습니다. 상황 설명과 목적이 원활하게 연결되면 질문이 3개 이하가 되어도 크게 결과에 영향이 없는 것처럼 보입니다.

## How to Answer

**Q1.** I am going to give you a situation to act out. One of your friends bought a new MP3 player that you were thinking of buying. Call your friend and ask 3 or 4 questions about his or her new MP3 player.

| 내용구성하기 | | | | |
|---|---|---|---|---|
| | Introduction | ✓ 전화 표현(인사) | | |
| | Body | ✓ 전화 목적 | ✓ MP3에 관한 질문들 | |
| | Closing | ✓ 전화 표현(끝인사) | | |

### Introduction

Hello, this is Christine calling.

### Body

I heard from Jane that you purchased a new MP3 player. The model you bought is the one I have in mind. ❶ **Do you mind** if I ask you some questions about it before I finally decide ❷ **whether or not** to buy it?

First of all, how much did you pay for it? What are some new features you noticed? Is it easy to use? Finally, can you tell me how you feel about the device? You have used it for several days now and I want your honest opinion. ❸ **Would you recommend** the device?

### Closing

That is all. Please call me back. Bye.

### Useful Expressions

❶ Do you mind…
~해도 될까요?
▶ Do you mind if I open the window?

❷ Whether or not
~일지 아닐지, 어떻든지
▶ You need to decide whether or not to go there.

❸ Would you recommend…
~를 추천하시겠습니까?
▶ Would you recommend this restaurant to me?

# IM2  IM3+

| | | IM2 | IM3+ |
|---|---|---|---|
| Introduction | | Hello, I am Christine. | Hello, this is Christine calling. |
| Body | 전화 목적 | I have some questions about your new MP3 player. | I heard from Jane that you purchased a new MP3 player. The model you bought is the one I have in mind. Do you mind if I ask you some questions about it before I finally decide whether or not to buy it? |
| | 질문 | How much is it? What are some of the new features? Do you like it? Tell me about it. | First of all, how much did you pay for it? What are some new features you noticed? Is it easy to use? Finally, can you tell me how you feel about the device? You have used it for several days now and I want your honest opinion. Would you recommend the device? |
| Closing | | Thank you. | That is all. Please call me back. Bye. |

IM1  IM2  ▶  IM3+

### Why IM1~IM2?

**01** 'I am Christine'과 같은 전화 표현을 잘못된 표현
  ▶ 올바른 표현인 'This is'로 변환해보세요.

**02** 상황 설명을 생략하고 질문으로만 구성된 답변
  ▶ 상황 설명을 추가함으로 답변의 개연성을 높일 수 있어요. 또한 질문에 이유를 설명하면서 질문의 타당성을 강화 할수 있어요.

**Q2.** I am going to give you a situation to act out. You have been invited to a community event by your friend. Call your friend and ask 3 or 4 questions about the event you will be attending.

| 내용구성하기 | Introduction | ✓ 전화 표현(인사) | |
|---|---|---|---|
| | Body | ✓ 전화 목적 | ✓ 행사에 관련된 질문들 |
| | Closing | ✓ 전화 표현(끝인사) | |

### Introduction

Hello, this is Christine.

### Body

First of all, thank you for inviting me to the charity event. I ❶ **am greatly honored**. Before I go, there are several questions I would like to ask you about the event.

Where will it be held? I have never been there, so if you have a map, please send it to me.

What time will the event ❷ **take place**? I do not want to be late.

Lastly, do I need to prepare anything for it? If there is anything I need to do, please let me know.

I am very excited to be a part of your charity event and to help out people ❸ **in need**.

### Closing

That's all. Please call me back. Bye.

### Useful Expressions

❶ Be honored
영광스럽다
▶ I am honored to be here.

❷ Take place
개최되다, 열리다
▶ The concert will take place in March.

❸ In need
어려움에 처한, 도움을 필요로 하는
▶ We need to help those people in need.

**Q3.** I am going to give you a situation to act out. You are planning to go on a trip and you need to reserve a room at a hotel. Call the hotel and ask 3 or 4 questions to reserve the room.

| 내용구성하기 | | |
|---|---|---|
| | **Introduction** ☑ 전화 표현(인사) | |
| | **Body** ☑ 전화 목적 | ☑ 예약 관련된 질문들 |
| | **Closing** ☑ 전화 표현(끝인사) | |

### Introduction

Hello, how do you do? Is this the Marriot Hotel?

### Body

I have something to ask.

I ❶ **am planning to** visit the area this weekend and I am going to stay there for 2 days. Since I am traveling with 2 other people, I would like to ❷ **book 2 rooms**.

Is it possible to reserve 2 rooms for 2 nights this weekend?

If it is, what rate will you ❸ **charge per night**? Is it cheaper to book the rooms online?

Also, one of my friends is a vegetarian. Does your hotel offer any vegetarian options?

### Closing

That is all I need to know. Please call me back. I will be waiting for your call.

### Useful Expressions

❶ Be planning to
계획하고 있다
▶ We are planning to go there.

❷ Book a room
방을 예약하다
▶ I would like to book two rooms for the night.

❸ Charge per night
1박 요금
▶ How much will you charge per night?

 **My Answer** — Use the expressions from the Key Information to develop your sentences.

– Introduction


– Body


– Closing

# OPIc 공략! IM3+

## UNIT 19

# 대안 제시하기

# UNIT 19 대안 제시하기

**OPIc 공략! IM3+**

## Learning Objectives

주어진 문제나 상황의 전말을 본인의 말로 바꾸어 설명하고, 그에 대한 해결책 및 대안의 옵션을 2~3개 정도 제시 할 수 있다.

## Frequently Asked Questions

- I am sorry but there is a problem you need to solve. You borrowed an MP3 player but you broke it. Call you friend, explain the situation and offer 2 or 3 alternatives.

- I am afraid that you have a problem. You were supposed to meet your friend but you cannot get there on time. Call your friend, explain the situation and give 2 or 3 suggestions.

- I am sorry but you have an issue to solve. When you arrived at the hotel, you realized the room you got was different from what you had reserved. Call a manager, explain the situation and provide 2 or 3 alternatives to fix this matter.

- I am afraid there is an issue you need to resolve. When you got home, you realized that you left your bag at the store. Call the store, explain the situation and offer 2 or 3 options.

- I'd like to give you a situation and ask you to act it out. You planned to go to the park with your friend this weekend. However, you found out the park is not open because it's under construction. Call your friend, explain the situation and give 3 or 4 alternatives.

- I'm sorry, but there is a problem you need to solve. Due to bad weather conditions, you have to cancel your plans to go to the beach with your friend. Call your friend and give your friend 3 or 4 suggestions.

롤플레이 유형 중 가장 난이도가 높은 질문입니다. 질문에서 제시된 문제상황 설명과 대안을 함께 제시해야 합니다. 따라서 상황 설명보다는 대안제시에 비중을 두고 자신의 입장에서 대안을 제시하도록 합니다. 일상생활 및 회사생활 관련하여 다양한 상황이 제시됩니다.

## Key Information

### 전화표현

Hello, this is 이름 calling.
안녕하세요, 저는 이름입니다.

### 상황/이유 설명

I called you to explain the situation regarding _____.
_____ 관련 상황을 설명 드리려고 전화했습니다.

I have some problems with _____.
_____ 에 문제가 조금 있는데요.

I cannot make it to the event/party because _____.
이벤트/파티에 갈 수 없게 됐습니다. 왜냐하면 _____.

▶ Cannot make it
~을 해내다. 라는 뜻
여기에서는 시간내 도착할 수 없다 라는 의미로 사용된다.

_____ was broken while _____.
_____ 하면서 _____ 이 고장났습니다.

_____ was damaged when _____.
_____ 할 때 _____ 가 손상됐습니다.

There is something wrong with _____.
_____ 이 뭔가 잘못됐습니다.

### 대안(상품이나 물건의 손상)

I will buy you a new one.
새로운 것으로 사줄게요.

I am going to pay in cash.
현금으로 지불할게요.

I want to exchange the product.
상품을 교환하고 싶습니다.

I would like to get a refund.
환불을 받고 싶습니다.

▶ Exchange
무언가 두개를 서로 교환하다 라는 의미를 가지고 있고

▶ Change
단순히 바꾸다 라는 의미를 가지고 있다.

▶ Make up to someone
누군가에게 보상하다 의미로 사용

▶ 부사절의 주어와 be동사는 생략이 가능하다. If possible은 if it is possible 에서 주어와 be동사가 생략된 형태

대안 제시도 중요하지만 주어진 문제 상황을 자세하게 설명하는 것에 더욱더 초점을 맞추어야 합니다. 2-3개의 대안에 너무 집착할 필요 없습니다. 문제 상황 설명이 충분하다면 2-3이하의 대안들을 제시하여도 괜찮습니다

## How to Answer

**Q1.** I'm sorry but there is an issue that you need to resolve. You borrowed a new MP3 player from your friend but you broke it. Call your friend and explain the situation. Then offer 2 or 3 alternatives.

| 내용구성하기 | | |
|---|---|---|
| Introduction | ☑ 전화 표현(인사) | |
| Body | ☑ MP3가 고장난 상황 설명 | ☑ 상황을 해결할 대안들 제시 |
| Closing | ☑ 전화 표현(끝인사) | |

### Introduction

Hello, ❶ **this is Ryan calling**.

### Body

First of all, ❷ **thank you again for** lending me your MP3 player, but there is a problem. I am so sorry to say that I broke it. I was riding my bicycle when I dropped it ❸ **by accident**.

I will go to the customer service center to get it repaired. If you do not want it repaired, I would be happy to buy you a new one. If neither of these options works, I want to pay for it in cash.

It is totally my fault and I really want to ❹ **make it up to** you.

### Closing

Once again, I am truly sorry. Please call me back as soon as possible.

### Useful Expressions

❶ This is … calling.
저는 ~ 입니다 (전화할 때)
▶ This is Ryan calling.

❷ Thank you for…
~해 주셔서 감사합니다
▶ Thank you for visiting us.

❸ By accident
우연히, 어쩌다가
▶ I bumped into the girl by accident.

❹ Make it up to…
(손해를) 보상하다
▶ I want to make it up to you.

# IM2 vs IM3+

| | IM2 | IM3+ |
|---|---|---|
| **Introduction** | Hello, this is Ryan. | Hello, this is Ryan calling. |
| **Body** — 상황 설명 | I had some problems with the MP3 player. I broke it. | First of all, thank you again for lending me your MP3 player, but there is a problem. I am so sorry to say that I broke it. I was riding my bicycle when I dropped it by accident. |
| **Body** — 대안 제시 | I am sorry. I will fix it for you. Or I will buy you a new MP3 player. | I will go to the customer service center to get it repaired. If you do not want it repaired, I would be happy to buy you a new one. If neither of these options works, I want to pay for it in cash. |
| **Body** — 사과 | | It is totally my fault and I really want to make it up to you. |
| **Closing** | Again, I am so sorry. Please call me back. | Once again, I am truly sorry. Please call me back as soon as possible. |

## Level Up⁺

IM1 IM2 ▶ IM3+

### Why IM1~IM2?

**01** 동일한 본문 첫 문장(앞서 질문하기에서도 사용했던 똑같은 패턴 'I have some questions/problems about...'으로 외운듯한 느낌을 주는 문장
   ▶ 다른 형태의 문장을 사용하세요.

**02** 단순한 문제 상황 설명 'I broke your MP3 player.'
   ▶ 상세한 문제 상황 설명과 함께 연관성 있는 대안을 제시하세요.

**Q2.** I am afraid that there is a problem you need to address. You are supposed to meet your friend but you cannot make it. Call your friend, explain the situation and offer 2 or 3 alternatives.

| 내용구성하기 | | | |
|---|---|---|---|
| | Introduction | ☑ 전화 표현(인사) | |
| | Body | ☑ 친구를 만나러 가지 못하는 상황 설명 | ☑ 상황을 해결할 대안들 제시 |
| | Closing | ☑ 전화 표현(끝인사) | |

### Introduction

Hello, this is John.

### Body

As you know, we were supposed to meet at 3 p.m. today. I was ❶ **looking forward to** it but there is a problem. I was driving to lunch when I witnessed a car accident. The police officer wants me to go the station with him because I am the only witness, so I think I need to go help him out.

I am really sorry about what happened. I know it may be ❷ **too much to ask** but can you wait for me? I can be there in about an hour.

If not, ❸ **why don't we** reschedule for tomorrow?

### Closing

Please think about what you want to do and call me back. Bye.

### Useful Expressions

❶ Looking forward to...
~를 기대하다, 고대하다
▶ I was looking forward to it.

❷ Too much to...
~는 무리다
▶ It's too much to ask.

❸ Why don't we...
~하는 게 어때
▶ Why don't we watch a movie?

**Q3.** I am sorry but there is a problem you need to resolve. You cannot find a website that your friend talked about. Call you friend, explain the situation and offer 2 or 3 suggestions to help you find the website.

| 내용구성하기 | | |
|---|---|---|
| Introduction | ☑ 전화 표현(인사) | |
| Body | ☑ 웹사이트를 못 찾고 있는 상황 설명 | ☑ 상황을 해결할 대안들 제시 |
| Closing | ☑ 전화 표현(끝인사) | |

### Introduction

Hello, this is John.

### Body

I tried to go to the website you told me about but there is a problem. I cannot find the right website. When I type in the address you told me, it links to a blank page. I think I may have a wrong address.

❶ **Do you mind** texting me the address one more time? I just want to ❷ **make sure** I have the right address.

Also, ❸ **if it is possible**, could you send me a screenshot of the site? It would be much easier if I had a picture of the page, so I can easily recognize it.

### Closing

❹ **That's all for now**. Please text me back. Bye.

### Useful Expressions

❶ Do you mind…
~해도 될까요?
▶ Do you mind opening the door?

❷ Make sure
확실하게 하다
▶ I want to make sure if it's OK with you.

❸ If it is possible
가능하다면
▶ Let me know if it is possible.

❹ That's all for now.
지금은 그게 다예요.
▶ That's all for now.

**My Answer** — Use the expressions from the Key Information to develop your sentences.

- Introduction

- Body

- Closing

# OPIc
공략! IM3+

UNIT 20

상황 설명하기

# UNIT 20 상황 설명하기

OPIc 공략! IM3+

## Learning Objectives

문제나 상황 설명을 누가, 언제, 어디서, 무엇을, 어떻게, 왜 (5W1H)에 기반해 답변을 구성하여 듣는 이로 하여금 그 문제나 상황의 전말을 효과적으로 이해시킬 수 있는 답변을 할 수 있다.

## Frequently Asked Questions

- I am sorry but there is a problem you need to solve. Your friend called you to pick him up within 1 hour but you can't because of your work. Call your friend and explain the situation.

- I am afraid that you have a problem. When you got home after work, the door was locked and you do not have a key. Call your family member and explain the situation to resolve the problem.

- I am sorry but there is an issue you have to solve. Your trip was canceled because of a severe rain storm. Call the rental car office and explain the situation to cancel your reservation.

- I am afraid that you have an issue to resolve. You put your waste out but your neighbor was upset because of it. Call your neighbor and explain the situation to resolve this matter.

- I am sorry but there is a problem you need to solve. A real estate agent has informed you that they cannot find an apartment in your price range. Contact the agent to explain your situation to find a new apartment.

롤플레이의 한 유형으로써 질문에서 제시된 상황을 다른 대상에게 구체적으로 설명합니다. 질문에서 주어지는 문제상황을 정확히 파악하는 것이 중요합니다. 질문 유형으로는 일상생활 및 회사생활 등 다양한 상황에 대한 것이기 때문에 상황에 맞게 설명하는 연습이 필요합니다.

# Key Information

### 전화표현

Hello, this is 이름 calling.
안녕하세요, 전 이름입니다.

▶ I called you라는 관계부사절을 중간에 삽입하여 단조로운 문장에 입체성을 부여할 수 있다.
The reason why I called you is...
가 원래 형태.

### 상황설명

I am calling you because _____.
_____때문에 전화 드립니다.

The reason I called you is because that _____.
제가 전화를 드린 이유는 _____ 입니다.

I need to tell you about a situation that _____.
말씀 드려야 할 상황이 있는데요.

There are some problems with _____.
_____에 좀 문제가 있습니다.

▶ -thing, -body, -one은 형용사가 뒤에서 수식한다.

Something strange happened to me when _____.
_____할 때 뭔가 이상한 일이 일어났습니다.

I realized that there is something wrong with _____.
_____에 뭔가 잘못 됐단 걸 깨달았죠.

### 전화 표현(끝인사)

Call me back as soon as possible.
가능한 빨리 다시 전화주세요.

I will be waiting for your call.
전화 기다리겠습니다.

I am looking forward to hearing from you.
답변을 기다리겠습니다.

▶ Look forward to 에서 to는 전치사로 그 뒤에는 명사나 동명사를 목적어로 사용할 수 있다.

롤플레이의 한 유형으로써 질문에서 제시된 상황을 다른 대상에게 구체적으로 설명합니다. 질문에서 주어지는 문제상황을 정확히 파악하는 것이 중요합니다. 질문 유형으로는 일상생활 및 회사생활 등 다양한 상황에 대한 것이기 때문에 상황에 맞게 설명하는 연습이 필요합니다. 주로 전화를 해서 상황을 설명하는 경우가 많지만 때때로 전화가 아닌 직접 해결해야 하는 경우도 있으니 주의해서 답변하도록 합니다.

## How to Answer

**Q1.** I am sorry but there is a problem you need to resolve. A phone you bought has some problems and you want to exchange it for a new one. Call the shop and explain the situation to exchange the phone.

**내용구성하기**
- **Introduction** ☑ 전화 표현(인사)
- **Body** ☑ 고장난 전화기와 관련한 상황 설명　☑ 전화기 교환을 요구
- **Closing** ☑ 전화 표현(끝인사)

### Introduction

Hello, this is Mark who bought a phone from you this morning.

### Body

I am calling you because of a problem with my phone. When I got home and tried to turn it on, it did not respond ❶ **at all**. ❷ **Now that I think of it**, I did not test the phone when I bought it at the store. I should have tested it right in front of you. Then, I would not have needed to make this call.

Anyway, since it was purchased from your store this morning and I did not do anything to damage the phone, it must have been broken when I received it. I would like to exchange it for a new one. I ❸ **will be visiting** your store at around 5 p.m.

### Closing

If there is anything you would like to tell me before I come, please call me back. Otherwise, I'll see you at the store.

### Useful Expressions

❶ At all
전혀
▶ I didn't know about that at all.

❷ Now that I think of it
지금 와서 생각해보니
▶ Now that I think of it, I was wrong.

❸ Will be -ing
~ 할 예정이다
▶ I'll be visiting your store this afternoon.

# IM2 vs IM3+

|  | | IM2 | IM3+ |
|---|---|---|---|
| **Introduction** | | Hello, this is Mark. I bought a phone today. | Hello, this is Mark who bought a phone from you this morning. |
| **Body** | 상황 설명 | I bought a phone but it is not working. I think it is broken, but it was not my fault. | I am calling you because of a problem with my phone. When I got home and tried to turn it on, it did not respond at all. Now that I think of it, I did not test the phone when I bought it at the store. I should have tested it right in front of you. Then, I would not have needed to make this call. |
| | 요구 사항 | It was broken before I opened the box, so please exchange my phone for a new phone. | Anyway, since it was purchased from your store this morning and I did not do anything to damage the phone, it must have been broken when I received it. So I would like you to exchange it for a new one. I will be visiting your store at around 5 p.m. |
| **Closing** | | That is all. Call me back. Bye. | If there is anything you would like to tell me before I come, please call me back. Otherwise, I'll see you at the store. |

## Level Up⁺

IM1 IM2 ▶ IM3+

### Why IM1~IM2?

**01** 상황 설명의 주된 목표인데 모호한 단어 'not working'를 사용한 단순한 설명
  ▶ 좀 더 명확한 상황설명 'does not respond' 제공, 상세한 앞뒤 상황을 추가로 설명하세요.

**02** 'Broken' 이라는 단어의 반복적인 사용.
  ▶ 구체적인 상태를 문장으로 서술. 'damage'등으로 다른 유사단어를 선택하여 사용하세요.

**Q2.** I am afraid that there is a problem you need to resolve. You learned that the repairman will not be able to fix your window until next week. Call the repairman and give 2 or 3 reasons why it is important to fix the window sooner.

| 내용구성하기 | Introduction | ☑ 전화 표현(인사) | |
|---|---|---|---|
| | Body | ☑ 방문하지 못하는 상황 확인 | ☑ 방문 수리를 꼭 받아야 할 상황 설명 |
| | Closing | ☑ 전화 표현(끝인사) | |

### Introduction

Hello, this is Hyun, the owner of the house on Gangnam Street.

### Body

I called yesterday to ask you to fix my broken window as soon as possible, but I ❶ **found out** that you cannot fix it until next week. I do not know the reason why you cannot come until then but I hope you can reconsider.

**Without** your help, my family will have to stay in our home without a window in the living room. As you know, it is winter, so it will be very cold and very uncomfortable. If it gets too bad, we are going to have to stay elsewhere and we will need to spend a lot of money on finding accommodation.

Please look at your schedule again and try to ❷ **make some time for** my family.

### Closing

I am truly ❸ **looking forward to hearing** from you. Thank you.

### Useful Expressions

❶ Find out
발견하다, 생각해내다
▶ I found out the problem.

❷ Make time for...
시간을 내다
▶ Please make time for my family.

❸ Looking forward to -ing
~할 것을 고대하다
▶ I am looking forward to seeing you in person.

**Q3.** I am sorry but there is a problem you need to resolve. When you arrived at your family member's house to help them with something, you realized that the door was locked and you had forgotten to bring the key. Call your relative and explain why you were not able to do what they asked.

| 내용구성하기 | | |
|---|---|---|
| **Introduction** | ☑ 전화 표현(인사) | |
| **Body** | ☑ 약속한 일을 못했던 상황 설명 | ☑ 다음날 방문 |
| **Closing** | ☑ 전화 표현(끝인사) | |

### Introduction

Hello, this is Henry.

### Body

The reason I called you is because of the favor you asked me to do. When I arrived at your house to water your plants this afternoon, the door was locked. ❶ **To make things worse**, I forgot to bring the house key. Since I needed to go back to the office, I could not return to your house today.

I am very sorry. I will go back ❷ **first thing in the morning** and water your plants.

### Closing

I hope you understand the situation. Call me back. Bye.

**Useful Expressions**

❶ To make things worse
설상가상으로
▶ To make things worse, I was sick.

❷ First thing in the morning
무엇보다 먼저, 맨 먼저
▶ I want to fix the problem first thing in the morning.

 **Use the expressions from the Key Information to develop your sentences.**

- Introduction

- Body

- Closing

# II

## 실력다지기

☑ **Part 4 돌발주제**

Unit 21 | 재활용
Unit 22 | 지형
Unit 23 | 은행
Unit 24 | 호텔
Unit 25 | 교통
Unit 26 | 기술
Unit 27 | 지역행사

# OPIc 공략! IM3+

# OPIc
## 공략! IM3+

UNIT 21

재활용

# UNIT 21 재활용

OPIc 공략! IM3+

## Learning Objectives

평소 재활용 활동에 대해 소개하고 우리나라의 재활용 하는 방법에 대해 이야기 할 수 있다.

## Frequently Asked Questions

- Tell me about the recycling system in your country.
- How do you recycle? Tell me about the steps of the recycling process in as much detail as possible.
- Do you have any memorable experiences related to recycling?
- Ask an apartment manager 3 or 4 questions about recycling.
- Have you ever faced any difficulties when recycling?

## Brainstorming

**Step 1** Brainstorm key words and expressions about the topic.
**Step 2** Use the words and expressions to brainstorm possible questions.

**System**
Q. Tell me about the recycling system of your country.

**Activities**
Q. Tell me all steps you take when you recycle.

**Recycling**

**Experience**
Q. Have you had any memorable experiences recycling?

**Change**
Q. Explain some changes between recycling in the past and the present.

# Key Information

## 재활용 시스템

**Korea has a very efficient recycling system.**
한국은 매우 효율적이고 효과적인 재활용 시스템을 갖춘 나라입니다.

**People put effort into separating their waste for recycling.**
사람들은 재활용을 할 수 있도록 쓰레기를 일일이 분류합니다.

**The Korean government has tougher laws compared to other countries.**
한국 정부는 다른 나라에 비해 엄격하게 규제하고 있습니다.

## 활동

**What I need to do first is _____.**
제일 먼저 할 일은 _____ 입니다.

**_____ is the next step I usually take.**
_____ 가 그 다음 단계죠.

**Some people might recycle a different way.**
어떤 사람들은 다른 방식으로 재활용을 합니다.

▶ May
허가 May I open the door?
추측 He may[might] be angry.
추측의 과거형 May[might] have + p.p.
He may[might] have been angry.

## 변화

**Previously, the recycling system in my country was _____.**
이전에 한국에 있던 재활용 시스템은 _____ 였습니다.

**People would/used to _____.**
사람들은 _____ 하곤 했었지요.

**Over the last decade, there have been a lot of changes made to the recycling system.**
지난 십 년간 재활용 시스템에 많은 변화가 일어났습니다.

▶ Decade : 10
Dozen : 12
Score : 20

**People are required to _____.**
_____ 해야 합니다.

일반적인 문제들 뿐만 아니라 롤플레잉 문제들의 출제 가능성도 염두 하여 학습해야합니다. 전반적인 재활용 시스템이나 절차 등의 사전 지식을 미리 숙지하여 대답할 때 망설임 없이 시작할 수 있도록 해야 합니다.

## How to Answer

**Q1.** I would like to know about the recycling system in your country. What steps do people need to follow? Is it a choice or something people must do?

**내용구성하기**
- Introduction ☑ 효율적인 재활용 시스템
- Body ☑ 분리수거 개념 설명 ☑ 재활용 쓰레기 처리 방식
  ☑ 준수하지 않으면 받는 불이익
- Closing ☑ 느낌 및 의견

### Introduction

Korea has one of the best-organized recycling systems in the world.

### Body

To throw out waste, people must separate their recycling first and buy a special plastic bag produced by the government to dump non-recyclable items.

We ❶ **are required to** separate cans, plastic, glass, and recyclable paper from other waste. Recyclables can be disposed of on a specific day of the week in a designated area. In my case, every Thursday, we ❷ **are allowed to** throw out recycling in two designated areas near my building. The recycling will be collected early the next morning with other items of the same kind.

❸ **Keep in mind**; if the recycling is not separated properly, for example, if glass is dumped into the plastics bin, the waste management company will not take it. This means that people have to suffer as waste piles up until the next Thursday comes.

### Closing

Recycling may seem like it is difficult and requires a lot of effort, but Koreans ❹ **are already used to** doing it.

**Useful Expressions**

❶ Be required to…
~하도록 요구되다
▶ I was required to wear business suit.

❷ Be allowed to…
~이 허용되다
▶ I was allowed to take a picture.

❸ Keep in mind
명심하다
▶ Keep your family in mind.

❹ Be used to…
~에 익숙하다
▶ She is used to working alone.

★ 전반적인 재활용 시스템에 관련된 내용만을 말하는 것이 중요하다. 자기 자신의 재활용 이야기가 답변에 들어간다면 이어 나온 문제와 비슷한 답변을 할 수 있으니 주의해야 합니다.

# IM2 vs IM3+

|  | IM2 | IM3+ |
|---|---|---|
| **Introduction** | I will tell you about recycling system in Korea. | Korea has one of the best-organized recycling systems in the world. |
| **Body** — 개념 설명 | Recycling system is really good in Korea. We have to collect recycling waste. | To throw out waste, people must separate their recycling first and buy a special plastic bag produced by the government to dump non-recyclable items. |
| **Body** — 처리 방식 | They are cans, plastic, glass, and recyclable paper. And we need to do this at home. And we can throw them out on a special day in a week. My house, it is on Friday. | We are required to separate cans, plastic, glass, and recyclable paper from other waste. Recyclables can be disposed of on a specific day of the week in a designated area. In my case, every Thursday, we are allowed to throw out recycling in two designated areas near my building. The recycling will be collected early the next morning with other items of the same kind. |
| **Body** — 결과 | But if people do not recycle well, cleaning people do not pick up the waste. And we have to stay with smelly waste. | Keep in mind; if the recycling is not separated properly, for example, if glass is dumped into the plastics bin, the waste management company will not take it. This means that people have to suffer as waste piles up until the next Thursday comes. |
| **Closing** | It is the recycling system in Korea. | Recycling may seem like it is difficult and requires a lot of effort, but Koreans are already used to doing it. |

## Level Up+

IM1  IM2  ▶  IM3+

### Why IM1~IM2?

**01** 여러 개의 단문 사용과 단문을 잇기 위한 반복적인 **and**의 사용
  ▶ 접속사 **and**의 사용을 줄이고 긴 중문이나 장문 혹은 다른 접속사나 연결사를 사용하세요.

**02** 부족한 문장력과 정보로 인한 짧은 답변
  ▶ 전반적인 한국의 쓰레기 시스템과 재활용을 함께 설명하고 단순한 문장을 앞뒤의 상황을 설명함으로써 긴 문장과 적절한 답변 길이를 완성하세요.

**Q2.** How do you recycle? What do you usually do when it comes to recycling? Tell me the steps you take when you recycle in as much detail as possible.

### 내용구성하기

**Introduction** ☑ 내가 하는 재활용 절차
**Body** ☑ 집에서 분류 범주  ☑ 재활용 쓰레기 세척 및 건조
☑ 재활용 쓰레기 처리 과정
**Closing** ☑ 느낌 및 의견

### Introduction

❶ **As I said**, all I need to do is separate the recyclable waste and take it out on the designated day.

### Body

In my house, we use four different sorting bags for plastic, cans, glass, and paper. We separate our recycling at home to avoid making any mistakes.

Whenever we have things to recycle, I clean the containers first. ❷ **In the case of** cans, glass bottles, and milk cartons, I wash them inside out to rinse off any remaining product. Then, I let them dry. That way, I can save them inside for a week without them beginning to smell.

Once Thursday comes, my father and I pick up a bag of trash in each hand and take the recycling out. When we arrive at the designated recycling area, there are four big bins for plastic, cans, glass, and paper. All I have to do is to dump the bags into the right bin.

### Closing

Knowing that I am working to reduce waste and help the environment, I feel ❸ **proud of** myself.

### Useful Expressions

❶ As I said
내가 말한 바와 같이
▶ As I said, I am very busy.

❷ In the case of…
~의 경우에는
▶ In the case of cans, I need to throw them away separately.

❸ Proud of…
~가 자랑스럽다
▶ I'm proud of my mom.

★ 일의 절차를 물어보는 질문으로 현재시제를 사용해야 하며 적절한 길이의 답변을 만들기 위해 세부적인 절차까지 설명하는 것이 좋습니다.

**Q3.** Do you have any memorable experiences related to recycling? For example, it could be about a time that you did something wrong or when the trash was not collected properly. Tell me about your experience in detail.

**내용구성하기**
- **Introduction** ☑ 새 아파트에서 경험
- **Body** ☑ 재활용 쓰레기 처리 장소 찾기   ☑ 지인과 만남
  ☑ 쓰레기 수거 실수 발생
- **Closing** ☑ 느낌 및 의견

### Introduction

About four years ago, when my family just moved into a new apartment, we were all very excited to move into a newly constructed building.

### Body

We ❶ **were informed that** we had to take out our recycling on Friday. When the first Friday came I took out the recycling by myself since there was not much waste. When I looked for the dumping place, I noticed another person taking out his trash.

As I approached the recycling area, I ❷ **felt like** something was wrong. It ❸ **did not take too long to** realize what it was. The person by the bins was my boss. He recognized me and it was very awkward. I ran back home as quickly as possible.

The next day, I saw a notice with a picture in the elevator. It said that the garbage truck did not accept the recycling bins from our building because they found food waste in one. I felt annoyed that somebody had made a mistake.

But then I noticed a somewhat familiar yellow t-shirt in the picture. It was me. I was so preoccupied with the awkward meeting with my boss that I did not realize I put the food waste into one of recycling bins.

### Closing

I ❹ **felt really sorry for** people living in my building because we couldn't get rid of our smelly trash for another week.

**Useful Expressions**

❶ Be informed that…
~라고 통지 받다
▶ We were informed that we had to move out.

❷ Feel like…
동사 하는데 얼마 걸리지 않았다.
▶ I felt like something was wrong.

❸ Didn't take too long to…
~하는데 오래 걸리지 않았다
▶ It didn't take too long for me to recognize him.

❹ Feel sorry for…
~에 안타까움을 느끼다, 딱하다
▶ I felt sorry for what I did.

★ 재활용과 관련된 내용의 경험을 이야기 하는 것이 중요하며 과거 시제 사용에 주의해서 답변해야 합니다.

 **My Answer** — Use the expressions from the Key Information to develop your sentences.

— Introduction

— Body

— Closing

# OPIc
## 공략! IM3+

UNIT **22**

지형

# UNIT 22 지형

**OPIc 공략! IM3+**

## Learning Objectives

우리나라의 지리적 특징 및 일반적으로 즐기는 야외활동 장소의 지형적 특징을 묘사하고 지리와 관련된 어릴 적 경험을 말할 수 있다.

## Frequently Asked Questions

- Tell me about the geography or landscape of your country.
- Describe a region that is geographically unique.
- Describe a place you would recommend for others to visit due to its special geographical features.
- Have you visited any places that are geographically unique?

## Brainstorming

**Step 1** Brainstorm key words and expressions about the topic.
**Step 2** Use the words and expressions to brainstorm possible questions.

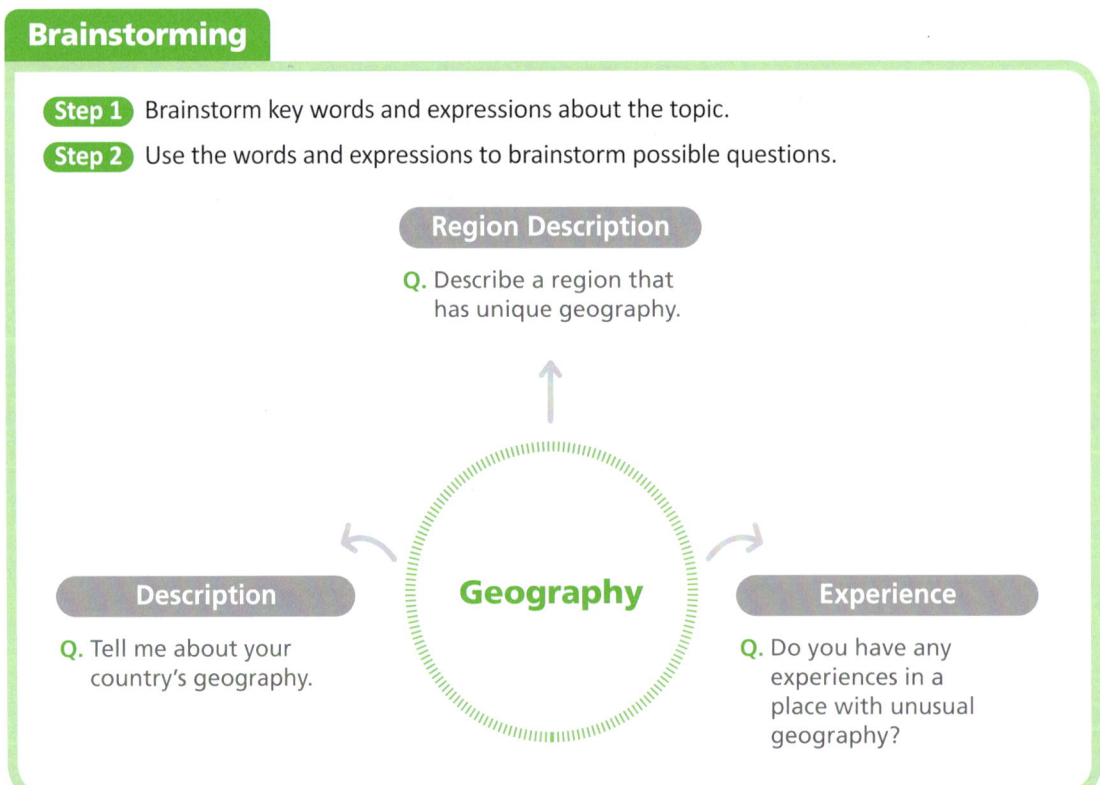

# Key Information

## 지형

My country is located on a peninsula.
우리나라는 반도 지형입니다.

It is situated between _____ and _____.
_____ 와 _____ 사이에 위치해 있죠.

A mountain range stretches from _____ to _____.
산악지대가 _____ 부터 뻗어 있습니다.

A river runs from _____ to _____.
강이 _____ 를 통과해 흐릅니다.

▶ 물이 흐르다에 사용되는 표현들
Run : 흐르다
Flow : 흐르다
Meander : 굽이쳐 흐르다

## 지형 설명

_____ can be found in _____.
_____ 에서는 _____ 를 찾을 수 있습니다.

It was formed by volcanic activity.
화산 활동에 의해 형성됐지요.

Special geographic features like _____ can be seen there.
_____ 같은 지형적인 특징들을 _____ 에서 볼 수 있습니다.

The most distinctive trait of the place is _____.
이 곳의 가장 뚜렷한 특징은 _____ 입니다.

▶ 비교급과 최상급의 사용
3음절 이상이거나 분사의 형태 또는
-ive, -ous, -ful 등으로 끝나는
형용사에는 more, most 사용.

## 경험

Once I visited _____ where _____.
_____ 에 있는 _____ 를 한번 가본 적이 있습니다.

I was so impressed that I would like to visit _____ again.
아주 깊은 인상을 받아서 _____ 에 한번 더 가보고 싶습니다.

▶ 감정을 나타내는 분사
감정을 느낀다는 의미로 사용 될 경우에는
과거 분사를 사용하여 표현

한국의 대표적인 지형적 특징을 서술하는 문제입니다. 첫번째 문제에서 특정한 지역을 세부적으로 설명하지 않도록 조심해야 합니다. 그 이유는 두번째 질문에 대한 대답이 반복적인 표현이나 중복되는 내용을 서술할 수 있기 때문입니다. 높은 수준의 지형 관련 어휘는 필요 없으나 기본적인 지형 관련 어휘를 알고 있지 않다면 매우 당황스러운 문제임으로 미리 연습해 보는 것이 필요합니다.

## How to Answer

**Q1.** Describe the geography of your country. Are there mountains? Does it have a coastline? Share all the details you can about the geography and landscape of your country.

| 내용구성하기 | | |
|---|---|---|
| Introduction | ☑ 한국 지형 소개 | |
| Body | ☑ 반도와 분단된 지형  ☑ 산과 산맥 지형  ☑ 바다와 섬지형 | |
| Closing | ☑ 느낌 및 의견 | |

### Introduction

Korea, my country, ❶ **is located** between China and Japan.

### Body

It is a peninsula surrounded by three seas: the East Sea, the South Sea, and the West Sea. Unfortunately Korea is divided into two countries. The northern part of the peninsula ❷ **is occupied by** the Democratic People's Republic of Korea and the Republic of Korea, my country, occupies the southern part.

Korea is a country with a lot of mountains and mountain ranges. It has a long mountain range called Taebaek that stretches from north to south like the backbone of Korea. There are mountain ranges that are ❸ **rooted from** it. Korea has eight provinces. The capital city, Seoul, is located in the middle of the Korean peninsula.

Korea has a lot of islands. Among them, three islands are particularly important. Jeju Island is the biggest island located in the South Sea. Dokdo Island is in the East Sea and is a very important island due to its role in the territorial dispute between Korea and Japan. Baengnyeongdo Island is in the West Sea and is the closest island to the Democratic People's Republic of Korea, so it has been the site of several military conflicts.

### Closing

Korea is a unique country with a unique geographic makeup.

### Useful Expressions

❶ Be located…
~에 위치하다
▶ It is located between two countries.

❷ Be occupied by…
~에 의해 점유되다
▶ The place was occupied by another country.

❸ Rooted from…
~에 뿌리를 두고 있다
▶ The mountain ranges are rooted from Taebaek.

★ 지형 문제는 단어들이 생소하고 발음이 어렵기 때문에 미리 준비하고 연습 하는 것이 필요합니다. 전문적인 정보를 줄 필요는 없으니 지형 관련 표현과 어휘에 집착하지 않도록 충분하지만 한국을 나타낼 수 있는 peninsula와 같은 단어는 사용하는 것이 좋습니다. 한 지역에 집중되지 않도록 주의합니다.

# IM2 vs IM3+

| | IM2 | IM3+ |
|---|---|---|
| **Introduction** | I am going to tell you about Korea's geography. | Korea, my country, is located between China and Japan. |
| **Body** — 분단된 지형 | | It is a peninsula surrounded by three seas: the East Sea, the South Sea, and the West Sea. Unfortunately Korea is divided into two countries. The northern part of the peninsula is occupied by the Democratic People's Republic of Korea and the Republic of Korea, my country, occupies the southern part. |
| **Body** — 산과 산맥 | It has three Seas and there is China in the West and Japan in the East. It is small country with a lot of mountains. It has rivers too, like Hangang River, Nakdonggang River, Imjingang River and so on. | Korea is a country with a lot of mountains and mountain ranges. It has a long mountain range called Taebaek that stretches from north to south like the backbone of Korea. There are mountain ranges that are rooted from it. Korea has eight provinces. The capital city, Seoul, is located in the middle of the Korean peninsula. |
| **Body** — 바다와 섬 | It also has many islands and Jeju island is the biggest island. It is very popular place to travel. There are beautiful beaches and very delicious dishes. Also it has special geography. There is a volcanic mountain. I actually went to Jeju island last summer and it was great experience. | Korea has a lot of islands. Among them, three islands are particularly important. Jeju Island is the biggest island located in the South Sea. Dokdo Island is in the East Sea and is a very important island due to its role in the territorial dispute between Korea and Japan. Baengnyeongdo Island is in the West Sea and is the closest island to the Democratic People's Republic of Korea, so it has been the site of several military conflicts. |
| **Closing** | It is the end of my answer. | Korea is a unique country and has geographic significance |

## Level Up+

IM1 IM2 ▶ IM3+

### Why IM1~IM2?

**01** 한글을 그래도 영어로 변환한 표현(Korea's Geography)의 사용
▶ 적절한 영식 표현으로 전환하세요.

**02** 한국의 지형보다 제주의 설명에 치우치고 있으며 경험까지 언급. 이런 답변은 전형적으로 다음 문제들과 답변이 겹칠 가능성이 높음
▶ 한국 지형에 대하여 전반적으로 설명하고 한 장소에 치우치지 않도록 주의하세요.

**03** 어느 문제의 답변에 사용할 수 있을 듯한 결론
▶ 주제게 맞는 결론으로 변경하세요.

**Q2.** I would like to know about a region that is geographically unique. Where is it? Why is it special? Tell me about it in as much detail as possible.

| 내용구성하기 | | |
|---|---|---|
| Introduction | ☑ 지형적으로 특별한 지역 소개 | |
| Body | ☑ 구멍 뚫린 검은 돌  ☑ 주상절리  ☑ 해안 폭포 | |
| Closing | ☑ 느낌 및 의견 | |

### Introduction

There are several geographically unique places I would like to talk about. Right now, I would like to introduce Jeju Island.

### Body

It is the biggest island in Korea and it is located south of the Korean peninsula. The most unique thing about Jeju Island is that it was ❶ **made by** volcanic activity a long time ago. Volcanic traits can be found everywhere on the island. First of all, its rocks are black and have a lot of tiny holes, which ❷ **are typical of** Jeju volcanic rocks.

Another geographical trait is the columnar joints. These are cliffs with a lot of column-like rocks. They can ❸ **be found** here in Korea.

My favorite geographic feature of the island is that there are beautiful waterfalls right beside the shore. The water from the falls goes straight to the sea and you can see rainbows whenever the sun is out.

### Closing

Jeju is a magnificent place. If you have not been there, I insist you visit the island as soon as you get the chance.

### Useful Expressions

❶ Made by…
~에 의해 만들어지다
▶ It was made by volcanic activities.

❷ Be typical of…
~를 대표하는
▶ It is typical of Jeju Island.

❸ Be found
발견되다
▶ The rocks were found on the beach.

★ 앞에서 언급했듯, 전문적인 수준의 어휘나 표현을 사용하기 보다는 기본적인 지형 관련 단어를 적절히 함께 사용하여 여행 장소를 묘사하듯 서술해 나가는 것이 좋습니다. 국내 장소뿐만 아니라 해외 장소를 묘사해도 괜찮습니다.

## Q3. Have you visited any places that are geographically unique? Where was it? Why did you visit there? What did you see? Tell me about your experience in detail.

**내용구성하기**

- **Introduction** ☑ 제주도 방문 경험 소개
- **Body** ☑ 동굴의 첫인상   ☑ 동굴의 다른 모습
- **Closing** ☑ 느낌 및 의견

### Introduction

I remember the time I visited Jeju Island about 10 years ago. It is a ❶ **well-known place for** many tourists.

### Body

The reason I chose Jeju Island was that I really wanted to visit the caves on the island. As soon as I arrived, I drove to a national park that contains a botanical garden and a cave. As I saw the entrance of the park, I ❷ **could not help but run** into the park. However, my first impression of the cave was a little disappointing. It was smaller than I had expected.

As I went deeper, I could see what ❸ **appeared to be** twinkling stars from above and beautiful sculpture-like rocks. They were so impressive that I decided to visit there again. I stayed in Jeju for four days and I revisited the cave on my last day. It was worth it.

### Closing

If you have not been there, Eva, I truly recommend you visit Jeju Island and see it for yourself.

### Useful Expressions

❶ Well-known for…
~로 잘 알려진
▶ The place was well-known for its beautiful beaches.

❷ Cannot help but do (something)
~하지 않을 수 없다
▶ She couldn't help but eat that cake.

❸ Appeared to be…
~로 보이는
▶ They appeared to be twinkling stars.

★ 과거 시제를 사용하여 문장을 구성하는 것이 중요하며 위에 언급된 지형적으로 특별한 여행지를 방문 했던 경험을 서술하여도 무방합니다.

 **Use the expressions from the Key Information to develop your sentences.**

- Introduction

- Body

- Closing

# OPIc
### 공략! IM3+

## UNIT 23
### 은행

# UNIT 23 은행

**OPIc 공략! IM3+**

## Learning Objectives

자신이 자주 가는 은행에 대해 묘사하고 은행에서 주로 하는 일, 은행의 편리성, 그리고 은행의 변화 등에 대해 말할 수 있다.

## Frequently Asked Questions

- Tell me about the banks in your country.
- What do bank tellers do? What are their responsibilities and duties?
- What kind of services do you usually use when you go to the bank?
- Have you recently had the experience of visiting a bank? What happened?
- What are some ways that banks have changed over the years?
- Ask a teller 3 or 4 questions about opening a bank account.

## Brainstorming

**Step 1** Brainstorm key words and expressions about the topic.

**Step 2** Use the words and expressions to brainstorm possible questions.

### Description
Q. Describe what banks are like today.

### Experience
Q. Tell me about an experience you had at the bank.

### Bank

### Activities
Q. What do people usually do at banks?
Q. What do bank tellers usually do?

### Change
Q. Explain some changes between banks in the past and in the present.

# Key Information

### 설명

Banks in my country play essential roles.
일반적으로 우리나라에서 은행은 중요한 역할을 합니다.

▶ Play a role
~ 역할을 맡다.

ATMs can be found near the entrance and a security guard is usually nearby them to offer any help.
입구 쪽에 ATM이 있고 도움을 제공하는 경비원이 그 근처에 있습니다.

_____ are available for the customers' convenience.
고객 편의를 위한 _____ 이 있습니다.

### 활동

A bank teller usually helps customers _____.
은행 텔러가 하는 일은 고객이 _____ 하는 것을 돕는 것입니다.

In my case, I often go to the bank to _____.
제 경우엔 _____ 하러 은행에 자주 갑니다.

Sometimes, banks offer special promotions to attract customers.
가끔 은행에서 고객 유치를 위해 특별 행사를 진행합니다.

▶ Promotion
승진, 촉진, 홍보 등의 의미를 가지고 있는데 여기서는 한글로 판매 촉진 이벤트 정도로 이해하면 된다.

If you do not know the process, you can simply ask any teller in the bank.
절차를 모르면 은행원 누구에게나 물어봐도 됩니다.

▶ If 의 조건절 사용
If 절 안의 시제가 현재이거나 미래이고 주절의 시제 또한 현재이거나 미래일 경우 가정법 용법으로 if 가 사용된 것이 아니라 주절의 사건이 일어날 조건을 나타내는 조건절로써 사용된다.

은행에 관련된 어휘를 잘 활용하는 것이 중점이 되는 문제들 입니다. 롤플레잉 문제들도 자주 나오니 미리 학습하여 시험을 보는 것이 좋습니다. 주로 등장하는 문제 유형으로는 자주가는 은행 묘사, 은행에서 주로 하는 일, 과거와 현재의 은행 비교하기 등 입니다.

## How to Answer

**Q1.** Can you tell me about the banks in your country? What are banks like? When do they open and close? Please describe a bank in as much detail as possible.

| 내용구성하기 | Introduction | ☑ 은행의 중요성 | |
|---|---|---|---|
| | Body | ☑ 은행 일반적 정보 | ☑ 은행 내부 묘사 |
| | Closing | ☑ 느낌 및 의견 | |

### Introduction

Banks ❶ **play an important role in** communities. There are many banks located throughout my country.

### Body

Banks open for business at 9 o'clock in the morning and close at 4 o'clock in the afternoon. Usually, banks are very busy all day long. It is not a pleasure to go to the bank because there is often a long line.

Banks in Korea look very stylish inside with ❷ **cutting-edge** security systems. A security guard is the first person you can see when you enter a bank. Beside the door, you can find ATMs. Inside the bank, there are long comfortable benches where customers can wait for their turn.

On the other side, there are counters and desks for tellers. When your turn comes, a teller may call you to come up personally or in big branches, your number will be displayed on a screen. At the edge of the room, there is usually a table with tea and coffee for customers to enjoy.

### Closing

❸ **That is all I can say** about banks in my country.

### Useful Expressions

❶ Play a role in...
~에서 역할을 하다
▶ He plays an important role in the community.

❷ Cutting-edge
최첨단의
▶ The company has cutting edge technology.

❸ That is all I can say
지금 내가 말할 수 있는 전부이다
▶ That is all I can say for now.

★ 은행에 대한 기본정인 정보를 답변하는 문제입니다. 자세한 묘사를 할 필요는 없습니다.

# IM2  IM3+

|  |  | IM2 | IM3+ |
|---|---|---|---|
| Introduction | | There are many banks and I will tell you about a bank in Korea. | Banks play an important role in communities. There are many banks located throughout my country. |
| Body | 일반 정보 | It opens at 9 and closes at 4. Banks are everywhere on the street. | Banks open for business at 9 o'clock in the morning and close at 4 o'clock in the afternoon. Usually, banks are very busy all day long. It is not a pleasure to go to the bank because there is often a long line. |
|  | 외부 묘사 | When you enter the bank, there are a security guard, bank tellers and ATMs. | Banks in Korea look very stylish inside with cutting-edge security systems. A security guard is the first person you can see when you enter a bank. Beside the door, you can find ATMs. Inside the bank, there are long comfortable benches where customers can wait for their turn. |
|  | 내부 묘사 | Also there are chairs for people to wait for their turn. And there is a table for free coffee and tea. | On the other side, there are counters and desks for tellers. When your turn comes, a teller may call you to come up personally or in big branches, your number will be displayed on a screen. At the edge of the room, there is usually a table with tea and coffee for customers to enjoy. |
| Closing | | It is a typical bank in Korea. | That is all I can say about banks in my country. |

## Why IM1~IM2?

**01** 묘사할 때 자주 사용되는 'there is/are' 구문의 반복적인 사용
▶ 다른 종류의 문장 구조를 사용하여 묘사를 진행하세요.

**02** 단지 사물만을 열거해 놓은 묘사 방식
▶ 형용사와 같은 수식어구의 사용과 사물이 있는 이유를 첨가하면서 좀더 세부적으로 묘사하세요.

**Q2.** What kind of services does a bank offer? Why do people go to a bank? Please describe the services a bank provides in as much detail as possible.

**내용구성하기**

| | | |
|---|---|---|
| **Introduction** | ☑ 은행 방문 목적 | |
| **Body** | ☑ 계좌 개설과 사용 관련 서비스 | ☑ 대출, 공과금 납부, 카드 발급 관련 서비스 |
| | ☑ 환전과 금고 서비스 | ☑ 상담 서비스 |
| **Closing** | ☑ 느낌 및 의견 | |

### Introduction

People go to the bank for many different reasons.

### Body

First of all, people go to a bank to ❶ **open a bank account**. Those who wish to open an account should bring a valid ID card with them. Once an account has been opened, they are able to use major banking services, such as depositing, withdrawing, and transferring money.

Banks offer loan services, which make it possible for people to borrow money with interest. People can pay their bills at a bank as well. Banks issue debit and credit cards, so customers can conveniently spend money.

Banks also provide currency exchange services for people who ❷ **intend to** travel abroad. For people who have precious items or important things to store, banks rent safety deposit boxes where they can keep their valuables.

Nowadays, banks offer consulting services as well, so people are able to discuss their long-term financial plans with specialists at the bank.

### Closing

Banks provide these services and more for their customers. I expect that the number of services offered will ❸ **continue to** grow in the future.

### Useful Expressions

❶ Open a bank account
계좌를 개설하다
▶ I would like to open a bank account.

❷ Intend to...
~할 작정이다
▶ I intended to travel abroad.

❸ Continue to...
~가 계속되다
▶ We will continue to grow.

★ 얼마나 많은 은행관련 어휘를 알고 있는지를 물어보는 질문입니다.

**Q3.** Could you describe how banks in your country have changed over time? Do you think they have improved over time? Please describe the differences between banks of the past and those of the present.

**내용구성하기**

- Introduction ✓ 현재와 과거 사이의 변화
- Body ✓ 기다리는 시간의 변화
- ✓ 손님에 대한 태도 변화
- Closing ✓ 느낌 및 의견

### Introduction

I have noticed several differences between banks in the past and now.

### Body

The first thing I have noticed is a huge improvement in waiting time. I remember that I used to wait at least 30 minutes whenever I visited a bank. Once it was so busy that I had to wait more than two hours. This was because even the simplest jobs, such as depositing and withdrawing money, had to be done ❶ **in person** at a bank. ❷ **Thanks to** ATMs and Internet banking, we are now able to transfer and exchange money as well as deposit and withdraw it without waiting in line.

Second, another difference I have noticed is the attitude of the banks. In the past, banks were scarce and there was not a lot of competition. They did not have to do anything special to attract customers. However, recently, competition between banks is so fierce that they must offer various benefits and promotions to promote their services.

### Closing

There have been many changes in the banking industry but ❸ **one thing is clear**. Things have become much more convenient for us consumers.

**Useful Expressions**

❶ In person
(사람이) 직접
▶ The job had to be done in person.

❷ Thanks to...
~덕분에, 때문에
▶ Thanks to ATMs, we don't need to wait in line for too long.

❸ One thing is clear
한가지는 분명하다
▶ While there are many problems, one thing is clear; there are also solutions.

★ 과거와 현재 사이에 차이점을 비교하면서 과거 시제와 현재 시제의 사용에 주의하세요.

 **Use the expressions from the Key Information to develop your sentences.**

- Introduction

- Body

- Closing

# OPIc 공략! IM3+

## UNIT 24

### 호텔

# UNIT 24 호텔

**OPIc 공략! IM3+**

## Learning Objectives

우리나라 호텔의 특징 및 자신이 가장 좋아하는 호텔에 대해 소개하고 최근에 방문했던 호텔 및 기억에 남는 호텔에 대해 이야기 할 수 있다.

## Frequently Asked Questions

- Describe a hotel you have stayed in before.
- What do you usually do when you go to a hotel?
- Compare two hotels you have visited.
- The room you are given is different from the one you reserved. Explain the situation and offer 2 or 3 alternatives.

## Brainstorming

**Step 1** Brainstorm key words and expressions about the topic.
**Step 2** Use the words and expressions to brainstorm possible questions.

### Description
Q. Describe a hotel you have visited in the past.

### Experience
Q. Do you have any experiences you can share about staying at a hotel?

### Hotel

### Activities
Q. What do you usually do when you stay at a hotel?

### Change
Q. Explain some changes between hotels in the past and in the present.

# Key Information

### 활동

As soon as I arrived, I _____.
도착하자마자 나는 _____ 합니다.

Soon after _____, I _____.
_____ 한 다음 나는 _____ 합니다.

Because I want to make sure my bathtub is clean, I wash it again by myself.
전 욕조가 깨끗한 걸 좋아하기 때문에 직접 욕조를 청소합니다.

_____ is what I occasionally do when I _____.
가끔 저는 _____ 할 때, _____ 를 합니다.

▶ As soon as 주어 동사
~하자 마자 의미를 가진 접속사이며
비슷한 표현은 아래와 같다.
The moment 주어 동사
No sooner A than B : A하자마자 B

### 예약

Is it possible to book a room for 2 guests for the 17th?
17일자로 2명이 사용할 객실을 하나 예약할 수 있나요?

Do you serve vegetarian meals?
채식용 식단이 제공되나요?

Do you offer _____?
_____ 를 제공하나요?

I would like you to tell me if it is possible to _____.
_____ 가 가능한지 알고 싶습니다.

▶ 간접의문문
Is it possible to...?와 I would like you to tell me 문장들이 간접의문문으로 한 문장으로 변환.
의문문에 의문사가 없으니 두 문장을 연결할 때 if나 whether를 사용하여 연결한다.
이 때 의문문은 평서문의 어순으로 바꿔야 하는 것 주의

기본적인 형태의 장소 묘사, 활동 그리고 경험 문제들로 기존에 학습했던 방식에 맞춰 답변을 준비 할 수 있습니다.
호텔에 머물렀던 경험이 없더라도 우리나라 호텔의 서비스, 가격, 음식 등에 대하여 묘사하는 것도 좋습니다.

## How to Answer

**Q1.** What do you usually do when you go to a hotel? Please explain all activities you do when visiting a hotel from beginning to the end.

| 내용구성하기 | | |
|---|---|---|
| Introduction | ☑ 호텔 방문 목적 | |
| Body | ☑ 혼자 방문했을 때 행동들 | ☑ 아이와 함께 방문했을 때 행동들 |
| Closing | ☑ 느낌 및 의견 | |

### Introduction

People go to hotels for many different reasons.

### Body

I primarily visit hotels when I travel. In this case, ❶ **the first thing I do** after arriving at the hotel is check in. If I am lucky, I can stay in an upper floor room with a view of beautiful scenery. After walking into my room, I always check if there are any ❷ **complimentary treats or teas** available for me. Then, I enjoy the treats and prepare for whatever I have planned for the next day.

When I go to a hotel with my kids I do things a little differently because they are young and they cannot walk around ❸ **as much**. If there is a swimming pool, I pack up our things and go down to the pool with my kids. If my kids are exhausted, we go up to the room and order room service. I usually choose to eat in the room with them so other guests can enjoy a peaceful meal without noisy children. At night, I take a shower and go to bed.

### Closing

These are the things I usually do when I stay at a hotel while traveling.

**Useful Expressions**

❶ The first thing I do
제일 먼저 하는 것
▶ The first thing I do is to take a shower.

❷ Complimentary treats or teas
무료로 제공되는 간식이나 차
▶ Hotels usually provide bottled water as complimentary treats.

❸ As much
그것과 동일한
▶ They cannot walk around as much.

★ 시간 순서대로 서술하는 것이 원칙이나 단조로운 답변이 될 가능성이 있으니 호텔뿐만 아니라 레스토랑이나 피트니스클럽 등에서 할 수 있는 활동을 함께 답변으로 구성하여 다양한 측면의 답변을 만들 수 있습니다.

# IM2  IM3+

| | | IM2 | IM3+ |
|---|---|---|---|
| **Introduction** | | I will tell you what I usually do when I go to a hotel. | People go to hotels for many different reasons. |
| **Body** | 혼자 방문 | When I travel, I stay in hotels. When I arrive at the hotel, I check in first. After checking in, I go to my room and take a rest. Then, I go out to look around. When I get back to my room, I have dinner. After dinner, I take a shower and go to bed. In the morning, I usually go to the hotel restaurant and have breakfast. I never want to miss it. | I primarily visit hotels when I travel. In this case, the first thing I do after arriving at the hotel is check in. If I am lucky, I can stay in an upper floor room with a view of beautiful scenery. After walking into my room, I always check if there are any complimentary treats or teas available for me. Then, I enjoy the treats and prepare for whatever I have planned for the next day. |
| | 가족과 방문 | | When I go to a hotel with my kids I do things a little differently because they are young and they cannot walk around as much. If there is a swimming pool, I pack up our things and go down to the pool with my kids. If my kids are exhausted, we go up to the room and order room service. I usually choose to eat in the room with them so other guests can enjoy a peaceful meal without noisy children. At night, I take a shower and go to bed. |
| **Closing** | | I think staying in hotels is a good experience. | These are the things I usually do when I stay at a hotel while traveling. |

**Why IM1~IM2?**

01  대표적인 말할 소재가 없어서 어려움을 겪는 문제. 역시 단순히 여행가서 숙박업소의 용도로의 활동만을 언급
▶ 단순 여행일 때, 아이와 함께 여행일 때 등으로 케이스를 구분하여 답변하면 문장수와 발화량 키워 보세요.

02  순서를 이야기 할 때 나오는 단순한 접속사 'when' 과 'after'를 주로 사용
▶ 다양한 접속사나 문장의 형태로 반복되는 단순 접속사 사용을 최소화 해보세요.

**Q2.** I'd like to know about a hotel you have stayed at or a hotel in your neighborhood. What does it look like? Why do you like that hotel? Tell me about it in as much detail as possible.

| 내용구성하기 | | |
|---|---|---|
| | Introduction | ☑ 호텔 이름과 장소 소개 |
| | Body | ☑ 호텔 외부 묘사   ☑ 리셉션 데스크와 레스토랑 묘사 |
| | | ☑ 홀과 헬스클럽 묘사   ☑ 좋아하는 이유 |
| | Closing | ☑ 느낌 및 의견 |

### Introduction

There is a 5-star hotel called HANKOOK Hotel located near my house.

### Body

The hotel has three buildings. One contains guest rooms, event halls, and restaurants. I feel like it is the real hotel. Another contains a duty-free shop, and the last building has a traditional garden for wedding ceremonies.

The main hotel building is 15-stories tall and has a large parking lot nearby. Its exterior is painted dark red and black so it can easily be seen ❶ **from a distance**. The hotel ❷ **is famous for** its high-end restaurants and luxurious ballrooms. When you first go in, you can see a reception desk where guests check in and out. The second floor is occupied by two high-end restaurants. One is a Chinese restaurant and the other is a Japanese restaurant. There are several ballrooms for special events on the 3rd and 4th floors. All the other floors have guest rooms except the 14th and 15th floors. A fitness club with a swimming pool is on the 14th floor and a rooftop bar is on the top floor.

My favorite feature of this hotel is its great restaurants. Whenever my family has a special event to celebrate, this hotel is our first choice.

### Closing

I believe it is the ❸ **perfect place for** any occasion.

### Useful Expressions

❶ From a distance
멀리서
▶ He could recognize me from a distance.

❷ Be famous for...
~로 유명하다
▶ The place is famous for its shopping center.

❸ Perfect for...
~에 안성맞춤인
▶ It is perfect for the wedding.

★ 기존의 장소 묘사 기법을 그대로 사용해서 이름/장소 ➡ 외부 ➡ 내부 ➡ 이유 순으로 답변을 효율적으로 구성할 수 있습니다.

## Q3. Have you had a memorable or unforgettable experience while staying at a hotel? If so, when was it? Where did you go? What did you do there? Why was the experience so memorable to you? Tell me about your experience in as much detail as possible.

**내용구성하기**

| | | |
|---|---|---|
| **Introduction** | ☑ 호텔 방문 경험 | |
| **Body** | ☑ 추락 사고 발생 | ☑ 병원 방문 |
| | ☑ 병원비 | |
| **Closing** | ☑ 느낌 및 의견 | |

### Introduction

About a month ago, I went to the HANKOOK Hotel to have dinner with my family.

### Body

My uncle's 70th birthday party was being held there and we were all invited. Although the service and the quality of the food far ❶ **exceeded my expectations**, there was a minor incident. I was with my 4 nephews and nieces. I ❷ **was so busy taking** care of them that I did not realize there were stairs in front of me. In a split second, I fell down the stairs.

I did not know what happened at first and I tried to ❸ **straighten myself out**. Then I felt a horrible pain in my arm and realized that I could not stand up on my own. Hotel staff ran up to me looking worried and took me to the closest hospital. After a few minutes, a doctor told me I had broken my arm. I had to get a cast put on my right arm. Before I could get upset, the hotel manager offered to pay for all of my medical expenses and even offered me some gift certificates from the hotel.

### Closing

I still have the cast on but I am deeply thankful to the hotel staff because not only did they pay for my hospital bills, but also they were very kind and eager to help me. I ❹ **was touched and moved by** their concern.

### Useful Expressions

❶ Exceed one's expectation
기대 이상이다
▶ The food far exceeded my expectation.

❷ Be busy -ing
~하느라 바쁘다
▶ We were so busy taking care of kids.

❸ Straighten out
~를 바로잡다
▶ I tried to straighten myself out.

❹ Be touched by...
~에 감동하다
▶ You were touched by their concern.

 **My Answer** — Use the expressions from the Key Information to develop your sentences.

- Introduction

- Body

- Closing

# UNIT 25

OPIc 공략! IM3+

교통

# UNIT 25 교통

OPIc 공략! IM3+

## Learning Objectives
우리나라 대중교통의 변화 및 장점에 대해 소개하고 교통과 관련된 경험 등에 대해 이야기 할 수 있다.

## Frequently Asked Questions

- Tell me about the different forms of transportation available in your community.
- Describe how you commute to school/work in detail.
- Have you had a memorable experience trying a new form of transportation?
- Have you noticed any changes in transportation between the past and the present?
- What are some issues or concerns regarding transportation in your community?

## Brainstorming

**Step 1** Brainstorm key words and expressions about the topic.
**Step 2** Use the words and expressions to brainstorm possible questions.

### Transportation
Q. What are some popular forms of transportation in your community?

### Activities
Q. Tell me how you commute.

### Experience
Q. Do you have any experiences taking public transportation?

### Change
Q. Explain some changes in transportation over time.

# Key Information

### 교통

The means of transportation available in my city are ＿＿＿.
제가 사는 도시에서 이용 가능한 교통 수단들은 ＿＿＿ 입니다.

Buses run to every corner of the city.
버스는 시내 곳곳을 운행합니다.

There are alternative forms of transportation in addition to ＿＿＿.
＿＿＿ 대신 대안적 교통 수단들이 있습니다.

People usually use ＿＿＿.
사람들은 보통 ＿＿＿ 을 이용합니다.

▶ **Mean** 의 여러가지 의미
동사: ~의미하다
명사: 의미, 평균
복수로 쓰이면 수단, 방법
형용사: 뒤떨어진, 비열한

▶ **Instead of...**
~대신에 라는 의미로 쓰이며 of가 전치사 임으로 뒤에 명사형태나 동명사 형태의 목적어라 자리한다.

▶ 교통수단을 통해서~ 라고 표현할 경우엔 관사를 사용하지 않는다.
By bus/subway 등.

### 활동

To get to work, the first thing I do is ＿＿＿.
출근 준비를 할 때 제일 먼저 ＿＿＿ 를 합니다.

I need to get on ＿＿＿.
＿＿＿ 를 타야 합니다.

After 5 bus stops, I transfer to the subway.
5정거장을 지난 후에 내려서 전철로 갈아탑니다.

I take a taxi if I am running late.
지각할 가능성이 있으면 택시를 타기도 합니다.

여러 형태의 교통 수단을 설명하고 관련된 어휘와 표현을 사용하는 것이 중요합니다. 자주 등장하는 문제 유형으로는 우리나라의 대중교통, 과거와 현재의 대중교통 변화, 교통과 관련된 과거 경험 등이 있습니다.

## How to Answer

**Q1.** Tell me about the forms of transportation you use most often. What forms of transportation are available in your area? Tell me about them in as much detail as possible.

| 내용구성하기 | | |
|---|---|---|
| **Introduction** | ☑ 한국의 대중 교통 시스템 | |
| **Body** | ☑ 버스  ☑ 지하철  ☑ 고속열차  ☑ 택시 | |
| **Closing** | ☑ 느낌 및 의견 | |

### Introduction

❶ **As you might remember**, I live in Korea. I can proudly say that Korea has one of the best public transportation systems in the world.

### Body

In most areas, buses, subways, and taxis are widely available. ❷ **Not to mention**, there are well-maintained roads for people who drive.

I live in a city near the capital, so I have all kinds of public transportation available in my area. Buses connect me to ❸ **just about** everywhere in the city and even other cities as well.

A subway station is located near my house. The subway goes directly to main areas where people tend to gather, so it is a convenient way to travel.

There is also an express train station called KTX that connects to cities located far away. Thanks to KTX, I am able to get to anywhere in Korea within 4 hours.

Since the roads are well organized, I can also easily find taxis.

### Closing

The greatest thing about using these forms of transportation is that I don't have to pay much. Public transportation fares in Korea are cheaper than most countries I have visited.

---

**Useful Expressions**

❶ As you might remember
기억 하실 지 모르겠지만
▶ As you might remember, I live in Korea.

❷ Not to mention…
~는 말 할 나위도 없고
▶ Not to mention, there are many fancy restaurants.

❸ Just about
거의 (다), 얼추
▶ I like just about anything.

---

★ 다양한 교통수단을 답변하는 것이 좋습니다. 하지만 개인적인 경험이나 일상에 관련된 대답은 다음 질문에 반복적인 답변을 할 수 있게 됨으로 피해야 합니다.

# IM2 vs IM3+

| | | IM2 | IM3+ |
|---|---|---|---|
| Introduction | | There are many transportation used in my community. | As you might remember, I live in Korea. I can proudly say that Korea has one of the best public transportation systems in the world. |
| Body | 대중교통 종류 | There are buses, subways, and taxis. | In most areas, buses, subways, and taxis are widely available. Not to mention, there are well-maintained roads for people who drive. |
| | 버스 | There are a lot of bus stops in my city and that means there are a lot of buses, too. I can go to almost anywhere in my city by bus. | I live in a city near the capital, so I have all kinds of public transportation available in my area. Buses connect me to just about everywhere in the city and even other cities as well. |
| | 지하철 | There are five subway stations in my city. One is close to my house. When I need to go to another city, I use this subway station. It is convenient and fast. | A subway station is located near my house. The subway goes directly to many areas where people tend to gather, so it is a convenient way to travel. |
| | 기차 | | There is also an express train station called KTX that connects to cities located far away. Thanks to KTX, I am able to get to anywhere in Korea within 4 hours. |
| | 택시 | I sometimes use a taxi if I am running late. I do not drive because of the traffic jams in the morning and evening. | Since the roads are well organized, I can also easily find taxis. |
| Closing | | I like my city because it has a lot of transportation options. | The greatest thing about using these forms of transportation is that I don't have to pay much. Public transportation fares in Korea are cheaper than most countries I have visited. |

## Level Up

### Why IM1~IM2?

**01** 'transportation'은 교통수단을 의미 하지 않음.
▶ 'forms of transportation'이나 'means of transportation'으로 바꿔 사용해보세요.

**02** 개인의 경험이나 일상의 정보를 함께 답변. 이는 다음 문제들이 비슷한 답변을 요구하기 때문에 반복되는 문장이나 내용을 말하게 될 위험성이 높음
▶ 개인적인 경험이나 일상을 최대한 배제하고 사실만을 답변하세요.

**Q2.** What forms of transportation do you use to get to school/work? Tell me about your typical morning routine and commute in as much detail as possible.

**내용구성하기**
- **Introduction** ☑ 통근 수단
- **Body** ☑ 버스 ☑ 지하철 ☑ 걷기
- **Closing** ☑ 느낌 및 의견

### Introduction

I mentioned before about the great transportation system my country has. This means that I can get to my workplace easily.

### Body

When I take the bus, I use a bus stop right in front of my house. With my smartphone, I can check when the bus is coming, so I usually wait 5 minutes or less.

When the number 7 bus arrives, I get on the bus. The fare is about a dollar. If I am lucky, I get a seat, but that usually does not happen. After 8 bus stops, I get off the bus to ❶ **transfer** to the subway. It takes about 15 more minutes by subway.

My office is located near the subway station. I just need to walk for about 5 minutes to get there. My workplace offers a direct shuttle bus from the subway station where I transfer from the bus but there are usually too many people waiting for it so I ❷ **prefer to** use public transportation.

### Closing

I enjoy my commute to work because I can listen to music or ❸ **collect my thoughts** while I travel.

### Useful Expressions

❶ Transfer to…
~로 갈아타다
▶ You can transfer to the subway here.

❷ Prefer to…
~를 선호한다
▶ I prefer to use public transportation.

❸ Collect one's thoughts
생각을 정리하다
▶ I can collect my thoughts on my way to work.

★ 다양한 교통 수단과 그에 맞는 표현들을 예를 들어 타다(get on), 내리다(get off) 등을 사용하는 것이 중요합니다.

**Q3.** When was the last time you tried a new form of transportation? When did you first use this form of transportation? Where did you go? What were you planning to do? Tell me about your experience in as much detail as possible.

| 내용구성하기 | Introduction | ☑ 제주 여행 | | |
|---|---|---|---|---|
| | Body | ☑ 비행기 이용 시기 | ☑ 불편했던 비행 | ☑ 무사히 도착 |
| | Closing | ☑ 느낌 및 의견 | | |

### Introduction

Recently, I visited my friend who lives in Jeju Island.

### Body

I remember the exact date. It was March 4th, which is my friend's birthday. ❶ **From where I live**, Jeju Island is pretty far away. But since it was her birthday, I decided to go.

The best way to get there is by plane. This was not my first time flying but it was the first trip I took where the flight was delayed. Because of bad weather conditions, the departure was delayed. Even after I got on the plane I watched heavy rain through the window. When it ❷ **took off**, I got really nervous because the plane shook really hard. I read books and magazines to distract myself.

Thankfully the plane ❸ **was able to** land on Jeju safely. I was going to give my friend a surprise party but when I arrived at the airport, I forgot about it because I was too tired due to the difficult flight. My friend was excited to see me and we had a great time together.

### Useful Expressions

❶ From where I live
내가 사는 곳으로부터
▶ From where I live, it is very close

❷ Take off
출발하다, 이륙하다
▶ The plane took off regardless of heavy rain.

❸ Be able to…
~할 수 있다
▶ I was able to come back soon.

### Closing

Since then, I always double-check the weather when am flying.

★ 특이한 교통수단을 사용한 여행 경험으로 답변한다면 여행 주제의 문제들과 함께 효과적으로 준비 할 수 있습니다.

 **Use the expressions from the Key Information to develop your sentences.**

– Introduction

– Body

– Closing

# OPIc
공략! IM3+

UNIT 26

기술

# UNIT 26 기술

## Learning Objectives

자주 사용하는 기술 및 기계, 장비에 대해 소개하고 과거와 현재의 과학기술 차이점에 대해 말할 수 있다.

## Frequently Asked Questions

- Tell me about the types of technology you often use.
- Tell me about the types of technology office workers/students use.
- Can you think of any differences between technology used today and in the past?
- Have you ever experienced difficulties because of technology?
- Your friend found a website that you are interested in. Call your friend and ask 3 or 4 questions about the site.

## Brainstorming

**Step 1** Brainstorm key words and expressions about the topic.
**Step 2** Use the words and expressions to brainstorm possible questions.

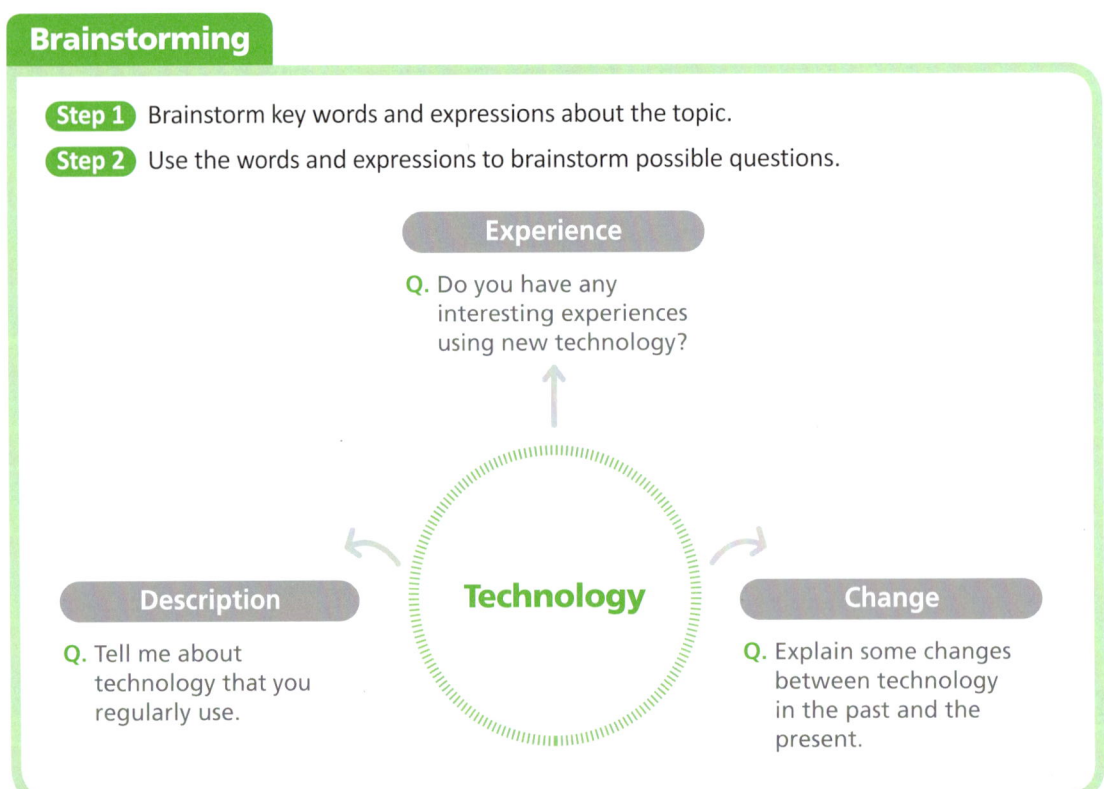

**Experience**
Q. Do you have any interesting experiences using new technology?

**Description**
Q. Tell me about technology that you regularly use.

**Change**
Q. Explain some changes between technology in the past and the present.

# Key Information

## 기술

What is commonly used nowadays is _____.
요새 흔히 사용하는 것은 _____ 입니다.

_____ are the most common types of technology.
_____ 은 요새 흔히 볼 수 있는 기술입니다.

The major reason people use it is _____.
사람들이 이것을 사용하는 이유는 _____ 입니다.

It helps people do things much more easily and faster than before.
이것 덕분에 전보다 훨씬 더 빨리 더 쉽게 할 수 있습니다.

▶ Help
준사역 동사. 목적적 보어 자리에 동사원형이나 to부정사 올 수 있다

## 변화

Although some changes are very obvious, people rarely notice all the improvements.
어떤 변화는 확연히 나타남에도 불구하고 사람들은 개선된 점을 거의 알아채지 못합니다.

The greatest difference I recognize is _____.
제가 깨달은 가장 큰 차이점은 _____ 입니다.

I believe these changes are usually positive.
이런 변화는 우리에게 더 낫다고 생각합니다.

▶ Although, Even though, Even if
비록 ~일지라도 의 의미를 가지고 있는 양보절을 이끄는 접속사.

▶ Rarely
부정의 의미를 가진 동사.
뜻: 거의~하지 않다.
유사어에는 **Seldom** 이 있다.

설문조사에 골랐던 문항과는 상관없이 내가 쓰는 기술, 학생들이 쓰는 기술, 그리고 회사원이 쓰는 기술에 대한 문제가 나올 수 있으니 대답을 구분하여 준비 할 수 있도록 합니다. 전문적인 수준의 기술 내용의 묘사나 서술을 필요 없습니다

## How to Answer

**Q1.** Could you describe how technology has changed from the past to the present? Do you think it has improved? Tell me about the changes in the technology you regularly use.

**내용구성하기**
- Introduction ☑ 기술의 변화
- Body ☑ 통신 분야의 변화  ☑ 음악 기기 변화  ☑ 교통 분야의 변화
- Closing ☑ 느낌 및 의견

### Introduction

I am ① **not an expert in** describing how technology has changed over time, but I can easily see that there have been distinctive changes in people's lives due to technological advances.

### Body

① **It is clear that** advances in technology help people enjoy their lives in a much more convenient way.

First of all, a few years ago, landline telephones and handwritten letters were pretty much the only ② **means of** communication we had. As computers, the Internet, and smartphones were developed, we can now ③ **keep in touch with** others constantly.

In terms of music, people used to be limited to cassette tapes and CDs but now no one needs to carry around bulky devices to play music. Instead, a smartphone has every function needed to enjoy music files.

④ **In regards to** transportation, there were not as many cars in the past and the public transportation system was not as well developed or as affordable as it is now. Nowadays, due to advances in public transportation, we can go anywhere at a relatively reasonable price.

### Closing

Advances in various fields have made our daily lives much more convenient and I believe that things will continue to improve over time.

### Useful Expressions

① Not an expert in...
~에 전문가가 아니다
▶ He was not an expert in cooking.

② Means of...
~수단
▶ It was the only means of transportation.

③ Keep in touch with...
~와 연락하고 지내다
▶ Let's keep in touch with each other.

④ In regards to...
~에 관해서는
▶ In regards to transportation, there have been many changes.

★ 기술의 발전을 효과적으로 설명하기 위해서는 답변하려고 하는 기술의 범위를 좁히는 것이 필요합니다. 예문에서는 통신과 오락 그리고 교통에 초점을 맞추어 서술하고 있습니다.

# IM2  IM3+

| | IM2 | IM3+ |
|---|---|---|
| **Introduction** | There are some differences between technology in the past and the present. | I am not an expert in describing how technology has changed over time, but I can easily see that there have been distinctive changes in people's lives due to technological advances. |
| **Body** 기술의 변화 | I want to talk about technology in the past first. | It is clear that advances in technology help people enjoy their lives in a much more convenient way. |
| 통신 | In the past, there was not as much technology available. Landline telephones were the most advanced technology available. Most people did not have computers in their homes. Everyone used cassette tape players to listen to music. People had to go to a movie theater to watch movies. | First of all, a few years ago, landline telephones and handwritten letters were pretty much the only means of communication we had. As computers, the Internet, and smartphones were developed, we can now keep in touch with others constantly. |
| 음악 | Now, we live a different life. People make documents using home computers and save them as files. Also, almost everyone has a smartphone. It can be used to call people, listen to music and watch movies. | In terms of music, people used to be limited to cassette tapes and CDs but now no one needs to carry around bulky devices to play music. Instead, a smartphone has every function needed to enjoy music files. |
| 교통 | | In regards to transportation, there were not as many cars in the past and the public transportation system was not as well developed or as affordable as it is now. Nowadays, due to advances in public transportation, we can go anywhere at a relatively reasonable price. |
| **Closing** | I think new technology is good for many people. | Advances in various fields have made our daily lives much more convenient and I believe that things will continue to improve over time. |

## Level Up+

### Why IM1~IM2?

**01** 'everyone'이나 'people'로 시작하는 비슷한 유형의 문장과 'available'같은 어휘의 반복적 사용
▶ 주어를 다양하게 사용하여 문장의 다양성 확보하고 뜻은 비슷하지만 다른 어휘를 사용하세요.

**02** 기술을 전반적으로 설명하고 있으나 범위가 넓어 과거와 현재의 차이의 관련성이 적고 맥락상으로 동떨어진 비교를 하는 느낌
▶ 기술의 범위를 통신, 오락, 그리고 교통으로 줄이고 이를 구체적으로 설명하세요.

**Q2.** What kind of technology do you think is most useful in daily life? What types of technology do you use most frequently? Why do you like those kinds of technology?

**내용구성하기**

| | | |
|---|---|---|
| **Introduction** | ☑ 스마트폰 소개 | |
| **Body** | ☑ 컴퓨터와 비슷한 기능 | ☑ 디지털 카메라로써의 기능 |
| | ☑ 오락 기기로써의 기능 | |
| **Closing** | ☑ 느낌 및 의견 | |

### Introduction

Of all the technology that people use every day, I think the most commonly used one is a smartphone.

### Body

It ❶ **combines many types of essential technology into** one small gadget.

We are able to make calls as well as use it like a computer to access the Internet. Visiting websites, checking e-mails, and searching for information can all be done with a smartphone. It is also possible to make simple documents with the right applications.

In addition, a smartphone can ❷ **be used as** a digital camera. It even has more advanced functions than a normal digital camera, such as the ability to edit pictures and movies right on the phone.

A smartphone can also be used as an entertainment center. ❸ **When it comes to** listening to music, it can be used as an MP3 player. It can also be used to play games and as a navigation system to help people find the best route to get to where they need to go.

### Closing

I think smartphones are essential devices for modern life and that is why a large number of people use them every day.

**Useful Expressions**

❶ Combine into...
~로 결합하다
▶ You can combine these into a single install.

❷ Be used as...
~로 사용되다
▶ It can be used as a digital camera.

❸ When it comes to...
~에 관한 한
▶ When it comes to listening to music, it can be used as an MP3 player.

★ 음악감상하기의 도구, 묘사하기 와 비슷한 맥락의 질문이므로 두 문제에 대한 대답을 함께 고려하면 좀 더 효과적으로 시험 준비를 할 수 있습니다.

**Q3.** Have you ever had any experiences when you had difficulties due to technology? When was it? What happened? How did you resolve the situation?

**내용구성하기**

| | | |
|---|---|---|
| **Introduction** | ✓ 8년전 경험 | |
| **Body** | ✓ 전화기 구매 | ✓ 요금 과다 청구 |
| | ✓ 나의 실수 | |
| **Closing** | ✓ 느낌 및 의견 | |

### Introduction

There have been several incidents that made me think that ❶ **I'm not good with** new technology. The most memorable thing happened about 8 years ago.

### Body

That was when the first smartphones were released in my country. Everybody was very excited to get one.

As soon as I got my phone, I was very into it. I took it with me everywhere I went. I ❷ **was amazed** at the unlimited uses for my phone. Sometimes I spent the whole day reading about new applications and different features that I could use.

However, my happiness did not last very long. When I got my first phone bill, I ❸ **could not believe my eyes**. I had to pay more than 200 dollars in data charges. I called customer service and asked what happened.

I thought it must have been a mistake but the bill was correct. I did not know that I needed to set up my phone to switch to Wi-Fi when a signal was available. I found out that I had gone way over my data allowance and had incurred a lot of extra charges.

### Closing

After the incident, I tried to use my phone more carefully.

### Useful Expressions

❶ Be good with...
~에 밝다
▶ I was good with technology.

❷ Be amazed at...
~에 깜짝 놀라다
▶ I was amazed at the bill.

❸ Can't believe one's eyes
자신의 눈을 믿을 수 없다
▶ I couldn't believe my eyes.

★ 컴퓨터를 사용하다가 멈추거나 꺼졌다는 내용의 경험은 공식 주관사에서 쓰지 않도록 권고하고 있으니 다른 내용의 경험을 준비해야만 합니다.

 Use the expressions from the Key Information to develop your sentences.

- Introduction

- Body

- Closing

# OPIc
## 공략! IM3+

**UNIT 27**

## 지역행사

# UNIT 27

## 지역행사

OPIc 공략! IM3+

### Learning Objectives

동네의 지역 행사 및 자신이 참여하는 지역 행사에 대해 소개하고 지역 행사에서 하는 활동 등을 이야기 할 수 있다.

### Frequently Asked Questions

- Tell me about some events or festivals in your community(neighborhood).
- Describe your favorite event or festival.
- Have you had any experiences participating in an event or a festival?
- What are some current issues or concerns in your neighborhood or community?
- You have been invited to an event in your community. Ask 3 or 4 questions about the event.

### Brainstorming

**Step 1** Brainstorm key words and expressions about the topic.
**Step 2** Use the words and expressions to brainstorm possible questions.

**Community Events**

**Events**
Q. Tell me about special events in your community.

**Description**
Q. Describe one of your community's events in detail.

**Experience**
Q. Tell me about your experiences at community events.

**Change**
Q. Explain some changes between community events in the past and the present.

# Key Information

> 행사

There are several events/festivals in my community.
우리 지역에선 몇몇 행사/축제가 열립니다.

An annual _____ is held in _____.
매년 _____ 이 _____ 에서 열립니다.

The event is for _____.
이 행사는 _____ 를 위한 겁니다.

On every 날짜, there is a festival/an event since it is _____.
매 (날짜)마다 축제/행사가 열리는데 _____ 였기 때문이죠.

▶ 날짜 말하기와 전치사
년도: in 2017
월: in January
년도와 월: in January 2017
년도, 월, 일: on January 3rd/on the 3rd of January   일은 서수로 표현

> 설명

Of the events/festivals I have mentioned, I think _____ is worth telling you about.
앞에서 언급했던 행사/축제 중에 저는 _____ 을 얘기할 만하다고 생각합니다.

_____ is considered very meaningful because _____.
_____ 는 매우 의미 있는 행사인데 이유는 _____ 입니다.

Some prepare _____ and others do _____ for the event.
행사를 위해 일부는 ~를 준비하고 나머지는 _____ 를 합니다.

People in my community know _____ and they want to be a part of it.
우리 지역 사람들은 _____ 를 알기 때문에 참여를 원하지요.

▶ Be worth -ing
동명사의 관용 어구
-ing 하는 것은 가치있다.

 Answer tips!

동네 지역 행사에 대다수가 참석하지 않으므로 실제 경험과 거리가 있는 문제임으로 미리 학습하여 시험에 대비해야 합니다. 질문의 핵심 단어가 4개(event, festival, community, neighborhood)임으로 잘 듣고 분석해서 대답해야 합니다.

## How to Answer

**Q1.** I would like to know about various events held in your neighborhood. What kind of events are held there? Tell me about the events you can see in your neighborhood.

**내용구성하기**
- Introduction ☑ 이벤트 소개
- Body ☑ 자선이벤트 ☑ 어린이날 축제 ☑ 보름달 축제
  ☑ 광복절 ☑ 벼룩시작 ☑ 정기시장
- Closing ☑ 느낌 및 의견

### Introduction

There are many events held in my community.

### Body

First, an annual charity event is held in December. Its purpose is to help people in need.

A festival for children ❶ **takes place** in May. There are many games and foods that children can enjoy.

A Full Moon festival ❷ **is held in** August or September.

For Independence Day, there is a special ceremony in the morning and fireworks at night on August 15th.

There are also flea markets to buy and sell used goods held ❸ **every quarter**.

Finally, once a week, there is a farmers' market right in front of my house.

### Closing

All of these are really exciting events. If you have never participated in any of them before, please come and experience them. I am sure that you will like them a lot.

**Useful Expressions**

❶ Take place
개최되다
▸ The festival takes place in May.

❷ Be held in...
~에서 열리다, ~때 열리다
▸ The event will be held in Korea.

❸ Every quarter
도처에서
▸ It happens in every quarter.

★ 질문에 events/festivals와 같이 다수의 동네 이벤트나 축제를 서술하라고 되어있습니다. 한 두개의 이벤트를 자세히 서술하지 않도록 주의합니다.

# IM2 vs IM3+

| | | IM2 | IM3+ |
|---|---|---|---|
| Introduction | | There are many events in my community. | There are many events held in my community. |
| Body | 축제 1 | The most popular event is a charity event usually held in December. It is the biggest event in my community. It is to help people. We donate money or buy some goods. I participated in the event last year and it was very meaningful. I plan to participate it again this year. | First, an annual charity event is held in December. Its purpose is to help people in need. |
| | 축제 2 | There is also children's festival held in May. May 5th is Children's Day. | A festival for children takes place in May. There are many games and foods that children can enjoy. |
| | 축제 3 | On New Year's Day, there is another event. You can see people wearing Korean traditional clothes called Hanbok. | A Full Moon festival is held in August or September. |
| | 축제 4 | Also, the Full Moon festival is usually held in September or October. | For Independence Day, there is a special ceremony in the morning and fireworks at night on August 15$^{th}$. |
| | 축제 5 | | There are also flea markets to buy and sell used goods held every quarter. |
| | 축제 6 | | Finally, once a week, there is a farmers' market right in front of my house. |
| Closing | | I think all these events are exciting. | All of these are really exciting events. If you have never participated in any of them before, please come and experience them. I am sure that you will like them a lot. |

### Level Up

IM1 IM2 ▶ IM3+

**Why IM1~IM2?**

**01** 이벤트에 대한 설명 뿐만 아니라 불필요한 개인 경험도 첨부되어 있는 답변
▶ 개인의 경험과 한 이벤트에 대한 설명을 배제하고 여러 이벤트에 대한 간략한 정보를 언급하세요.

**02** 'and' 와 'also' 를 반복적으로 사용하여 연결되어 있는 문장들
▶ 다양한 연결사를 사용하고 'and'나 'also'의 반복적 사용을 최소화 하세요.

**Q2.** Out of all the events you have ever been to, tell me about the most memorable one. What was the event about? What kind of things could you see there? Explain the event in as much detail as possible.

**내용구성하기**

| | | |
|---|---|---|
| Introduction | ☑ 자선이벤트 | |
| Body | ☑ 이벤트가 열리는 시기 | ☑ 이벤트 내용 |
| | ☑ 이벤트 참여하는 이유 | |
| Closing | ☑ 느낌 및 의견 | |

### Introduction

Out of all the events I've been to, I love participating in my neighborhood charity event the most.

### Body

❶ **As mentioned before**, it is usually held around December at a community hall, which is open to people in my community.

In December, each member of the community does something to prepare for the Christmas Bazaar. Some cook special holiday dishes and others make different handmade goods. I usually bring used clothes and shoes to sell. All the profits are donated to non-profit organizations to help ❷ **people in need**. Money is donated to a different organization every year. Last year, it was donated to the Children's Hospital.

People know every penny is ❸ **for a good cause**, so they all want to be a part of the bazaar.

### Closing

I am very proud to be a part of this event.

### Useful Expressions

❶ As mentioned before
앞서 말했듯이
▶ As mentioned before, I know him.

❷ People in need
앞서 말했듯이
▶ As mentioned before, I know him.

❸ Be for a good cause
좋은 일을 하기 위해서다
▶ Every penny is for a good cause.

★ 위에 언급되었던 이벤트나 축제 중에 하나를 선택하여 상세 묘사하는 질문입니다. 만약 대답이 짧다면 꼭 하나가 아니라 2개의 이벤트를 묘사하여 답변을 길게 만들 수 있습니다.

## Q3. I would like you to tell me about an unforgettable event you participated in. What was the event about? When was it? Why was it so memorable to you? Tell me about it in as much detail as possible.

**내용구성하기**

- **Introduction** ☑ 경험 소개
- **Body** ☑ 시간과 장소  ☑ 평소의 불꽃놀이 행사
  ☑ 불꽃놀이 관련 해프닝
- **Closing** ☑ 느낌 및 의견

### Introduction

I had a very interesting experience involving a community event.

### Body

Independence Day is a big holiday in my community. In the morning, there is a ceremony ❶ **in honor of** the people who sacrificed themselves for our country and at night, there is a huge fireworks display.

Two years ago, everything went ❷ **as usual**. We had a very solemn ceremony in the morning and when the sun set, people started to gather together in the community square to enjoy the fireworks. The fireworks display usually starts at 8 and finishes around 8:20.

But that day, something went wrong. Around 8, the sky suddenly became as bright as day with a very loud bang. After that, we did not see any fireworks. It was all over in 20 seconds. I heard what happened the next day. Due to a technical problem, all the fireworks exploded at the same time.

The following year, the fireworks were even more magnificent in order to ❸ **compensate for** the mistake made the previous year.

### Closing

But everyone still remembers the day we enjoyed twenty minutes of fireworks in twenty seconds.

---

**Useful Expressions**

❶ In honor of…
~에게 경의를 표하다
▶ The ceremony is in honor of the people who were killed during the war.

❷ As usual
늘 그렇듯이
▶ I was on my way home as usual.

❸ Compensate for
보답으로
▶ It was even more difficult to compensate for the mistake.

---

★ 경험 문제를 서술 할 때에는 과거 시제를 정확히 사용하고 있는지가 제일 중요합니다.

 **My Answer** Use the expressions from the Key Information to develop your sentences.

— Introduction

— Body

— Closing

# 실전 OPIc

☑ Actual Test 1
☑ Actual Test 2

# ACTUAL TEST 1

**Q1** Tell me about yourself and what you usually do on the weekends.

**Q2** Describe the geography of your country. Are there mountains? Is there a coastline? Are there lakes? Talk about the details of the geography and the landscape of your country.

**Q3** I would like to know about a region that is geographically special. Where is it? Why is it special? Tell me about it in as much detail as possible.

**Q4** Have you ever been to a place that is geographically unique or special? Where was it? Why did you visit there? What did you see?

**Q5** You said in the survey that you enjoy going to a park. I would like to know about the park that you usually go to. What is the name of the park? Why is it so special to you? What can you see there? Tell me about the park in as much detail as possible.

**Q6** What do you usually do at a park? What kind of activities do you usually do? Who do you do the activities with? Tell me about your routine when you go to the park.

**Q7** When was the last time you visited a park? Where did you go? What happened? Were you with anyone else? Please tell me everything about it.

**Q8** Tell me about a healthy person you know. What does he or she look like? What kind of food does he or she like to eat? How did you meet him or her?

**Q9** If you wanted to be a healthy person, how would you spend your daily life? What type of activities would you have to do every day? What kind of food would you need to eat? Tell me in detail.

**Q10** Have you ever done anything to be a healthy person? What did you do? What did you eat? Tell me your experience in as much detail as possible.

**Q11** I will give you a situation to act out. You are planning to travel and would like to rent a car. Call a rental car agency and ask 3 or 4 questions about renting a car.

**Q12** I am afraid that there is a problem you need to resolve. The travel agency called and told you your trip has been canceled. Call your friend, explain the situation, and offer 2 or 3 alternatives.

**Q13** Have you ever had any difficulties while planning your trip? When was it? Where did you want to go? What happened? How did you resolve the situation? Tell me about it from the beginning to the end.

**Q14** I would like to know the difference you think exists between Korean dishes and dishes from other countries. Are there any similarities as well? Compare the dishes in as much detail as possible.

**Q15** Have you ever heard any issues related to water shortage and food shortage around the world? Have you ever thought about them? Tell me your opinions on these issues in detail.

# ACTUAL TEST 2

**Q1** Tell me about yourself and what you usually do on the weekends.

**Q2** You indicated that you like to listen to music. What type of music do you like? When and how often do you listen to music? Who do you like to listen to? Why do you like them?

**Q3** When did you first become interested in music? Did anyone influence your musical preference? Do you still listen to the same kind of music you listened to as a child? If not, how have your preferences changed?

**Q4** Do you have any unexpected or special memories from when you went to a concert? Whose concert was it? When did you go? What happened? Why was it so special to you? Explain your experience in detail.

**Q5** Could you tell me about the banks in your country? When does it open and close? What does it look like? Where is it located? Also, please describe the people who work at the banks.

**Q6** Could you describe how the banks in your country have changed? Do you think it has been developed in a better way or not? Please find the differences between the past and the present in as much detail as possible.

**Q7** Please tell me about the last time you went to a bank. Which bank did you go to? Why do you prefer this bank? When was it and why did you go there? How long did take you to get everything done? Tell me about everything in detail.

**Q8** I would like to know about your house. What does it look like? What about your room? What can you see there? Describe your house and your room in detail.

**Q9** Compare the house you used to live in and the one you are living in now. What are some differences and similarities? Tell me with a lot of details.

**Q10** Have you ever done anything special at home? What did you do? Tell me about your experience in as much detail as possible.

**Q11** I'll give you a certain situation to act out. Let's assume that you have a toothache. Call the dentist's office and ask 3 or 4 questions to make an appointment.

**Q12** I'm afraid that there is a problem you have to solve. You are supposed to go to the dentist tomorrow. But you cannot keep the appointment and you can only go there next week. Call the dentist's office, explain the situation and give 2 different options.

**Q13** Have you canceled or delayed an important appointment? Why did you do so? How did you resolve the situation?

**Q14** I would like to know some differences between a trip that you took in the past and one that you would take now. Tell me with a lot of details.

**Q15** Experts say that it is important to take vacations. What do you think about this opinion? Do you agree or disagree? Give detailed reasons.

# OPIc 공략! IM3+

#  IV

## 부록

# IM-IH 학습가이드

## Strategies for Progressing from Intermediate Mid to Intermediate High

| Intermediate Mid (IM) | Intermediate High (IH) |
|---|---|
| A rating of Intermediate Mid indicates that the Speaker is able to:<br><br>• fulfill all of the requirements for the Intermediate level (creates with language by asking and answering questions about familiar topics, in sentences and strings of sentences).<br>• produce Intermediate level responses with both quantity and quality.<br>• produce responses that are consistently strong across all the Intermediate level assessment criteria. | A rating of Intermediate High indicates that the Speaker is:<br><br>• able to demonstrate the ability to function at the Advanced level most of the time.<br>• unable to sustain Advanced-level across <u>all rating criteria</u> all of the time. |
| **Intermediate Mid** speakers are at ease when performing Intermediate-level tasks and do so with significant quality and quantity of Intermediate language. They are able to express themselves by creating with the language, in part by combining and recombining known elements and conversational input to produce responses typically consisting of sentences and strings of sentences. Their speech may contain pauses, reformulations, and self-corrections as they search for adequate vocabulary and appropriate language forms to express themselves. In spite of the possible limitations in their vocabulary, pronunciation, and syntax, they are generally understood by sympathetic interlocutors accustomed to dealing with non-natives. | **Intermediate High** speakers operate at the advanced level most of the time, but have breakdown in one or more features of the Advanced level. Breakdown can be, among other things, failure to perform the required functions of the Advanced level, inability to maintain the appropriate time frame when narrating and/or describing about past/future (for example, reverting to present when talking about the past); failure to speak consistently in paragraph form when required by the function; or issues with accuracy so that the message becomes confusing for listeners (this may include weaknesses in pronunciation). |

**Strategies for Progressing from Intermediate Mid to Intermediate High**
(Note: A speaker at Intermediate Mid should start focusing on developing Advanced-level language. The Intermediate High rating indicates that a speaker is functioning at the Advanced level, but not all of the time. The strategies for progressing to IH will be similar to the strategies for progressing to A.)

1. Tell stories. Be sure to tell the whole story from beginning to end. Use words and phrases that support the chronology of your story. With a conversational partner, practice explaining and/or clarifying specific narrations and descriptions so that the listener is not in any way confused about the chronology of events.

2. Use appropriate verb forms to maintain descriptions and narrations in past, present, and future time.

3. Do not avoid situations in which you must resolve a situation with an unexpected turn of events (e.g. a lost wallet, a missed airplane, locked door, etc.) Role play practice is particularly helpful in developing strategies to "think on your feet."

4. Use connecting words (and, but, also, however, first, next, in addition, etc.) within and between sentences to produce oral paragraphs. These connectors (and others) can help you to develop greater clarity, organization, and detail in your speech.

5. Talk about familiar people, places, objects, buildings, cities, etc. using as much language as you can. Elaborate by including as much detail as you can. Use dependent clauses to add richness to your descriptions. Describe in a way that "paints a picture" for the listener.

6. Keep a written journal in which you record interesting observations, events, both personal and of a more general nature (e.g., current events in your community, city, country, etc.) Identify new vocabulary and phrases that are necessary to talk about these events. First write notes about the events, then practice telling them to a conversational partner while only referring to your notes, and ultimately doing so without using your notes at all.

7. Increase exposure to target language media (news broadcasts constitute excellent examples of narrations and descriptions in the past). Talk about what you have heard about reported on the radio or TV.

8. Read newspapers, magazines, and books in the target language. Retell events you have read about and that are of general interest.

9. If possible, participate in immersion experiences in English at home or abroad. The more "time on task," performing real-world functions across a variety of contexts in the language, the more likely you will achieve Advanced-level proficiency.

10. Work with a conversation partner or tutor who is familiar with your proficiency goals and the criteria for the Advanced level of speaking proficiency. Your conversation partner should provide opportunities for you to speak extemporaneously. Keep in mind that Advanced level speech is that which is produced by a full conversational partner. It is not rehearsed or prepared speech.

11. Work to improve pronunciation and intonation so that you can be understood by speakers of English who are not accustomed to interacting with learners.

12. Work to improve pronunciation and intonation so that you can be understood by other speakers of the language who are not accustomed to interacting with learners.

# OPIc 가이드 라인

American Council on the Teaching of Foreign Languages Oral Proficiency Ratings*
Brief Summary of OPIc Ratings(NH to A)
American Council on the Teaching of Foreign Languages

### Novice High (NH)

**A rating of Novice High indicates that the Speaker is:**

- able to demonstrate the ability to function at the Intermediate level most of the time.
- unable to sustain Intermediate level across <u>all rating criteria</u> all of the time.

**Novice High** speakers operate at the Intermediate level most of the time, but have breakdown in one or more features of the Intermediate level. Breakdown can be, among other things, failure to perform the required functions of the Intermediate level, such as the inability to create with the language (make their own personalized meaning) across a limited range of everyday topics; failure to use simple sentences consistently when required by the function; or issues with pronunciation and accuracy so that the message becomes confusing for listeners.

### Intermediate Low (IL)

**A rating of Intermediate Low indicates that the Speaker is able to:**

- fulfill all of the requirements for the Intermediate level (creates with language by asking and answering questions about familiar topics, in sentences and strings of sentences).
- produce Intermediate level responses but struggles to do so
- communicate primarily by using what they have practiced and hear from their interlocutors.

**Intermediate Low** speakers are able to perform Intermediate-level tasks, albeit barely. They are able to express themselves by creating with the language, primarily by combining and recombining known elements (what they have learned) and conversational input to produce responses typically consisting of short, discrete sentences. Their responses are often filled with hesitancy and inaccuracies as they search for the appropriate vocabulary and linguistic forms. Their speech is characterized by frequent pauses. Their language, including pronunciation, is strongly influenced by their first language, and therefore can generally be understood by sympathetic interlocutors, especially those accustomed to dealing with learners.

## Intermediate Mid (IM)

**A rating of Intermediate Mid indicates that the Speaker is able to:**

- fulfill all of the requirements for the Intermediate level (creates with language by asking and answering questions about familiar topics, in sentences and strings of sentences).
- produce Intermediate level responses with both quantity and quality.
- produce responses that are consistently strong across all the Intermediate level assessment criteria.

**Intermediate Mid** speakers are at ease when performing Intermediate-level tasks and do so with significant quality and quantity of Intermediate language. They are able to express themselves by creating with the language, in part by combining and recombining known elements and conversational input to produce responses typically consisting of sentences and strings of sentences. Their speech may contain pauses, reformulations, and self-corrections as they search for adequate vocabulary and appropriate language forms to express themselves. In spite of the possible limitations in their vocabulary, pronunciation, and syntax, they are generally understood by sympathetic interlocutors accustomed to dealing with non-natives.

## Intermediate High (IH)

**A rating of Intermediate High indicates that the Speaker is:**

- able to demonstrate the ability to function at the Advanced level most of the time.
- unable to sustain Advanced-level across all rating criteria all of the time.

**Intermediate High** speakers operate at the advanced level most of the time, but have breakdown in one or more features of the Advanced level. Breakdown can be, among other things, failure to perform the required functions of the Advanced level, inability to maintain the appropriate time frame when narrating and/or describing about past/future (for example, reverting to present when talking about the past); failure to speak consistently in paragraph form when required by the function; or issues with accuracy so that the message becomes confusing for listeners (this may include weaknesses in pronunciation).

## Advanced (A)

**A rating of Advanced indicates that the Speakers is able to:**

- narrate and describe in all major time frames in order to have conversations about both personal experiences, as well as topics related to community interest.
- handle a routine situation with an unexpected complication.
- produce paragraph-length or connected discourse when narrating and describing about a variety of topics.
- esolve a routine social transaction with an unanticipated complication.

**Advanced-level** speakers are consistently understood by native speakers who have no experience dealing with non-native speakers of the language being assessed. In other words, their message does not become lost, though this may occasionally require repetition or restatement.

# OPIc 금지답변

The OPIc is a test of spoken language proficiency. Proficiency is defined as the ability to use spoken language for real world purposes in order to engage in a spontaneous communicative exchange. Using recited responses during an OPIc does not provide sufficient evidence of language proficiency for a rater to assign an ACTFL proficiency rating. Recited responses are defined as entire passages that have been scripted, memorized and then reproduced during the OPIc.

The OPIc is rated by human raters who are trained to listen for patterns of strengths and patterns of weakness. The language you produce throughout the test is rated holistically according to the ACTFL Proficiency Guidelines 2012 – Speaking. Raters expect to hear personalized responses that address both the topic and the question asked. Raters do not expect perfection at any level. They recognize that as one is learning a language, spontaneous responses may contain imperfections and irregularities.

OPIc raters are also trained to recognize language that is pre-scripted and recited from memory during the test. The use of scripted responses that are recited from memory will negatively impact your rating.

What does it mean to be rated Novice High for recited memorized responses? Consistent use of memorized material is a function of the Novice level. If you wish to receive a rating above Novice, you must demonstrate the ability to communicate on a range of topics in your own words. You must create with the language in order to participate in genuine communicative conversations. If you consistently recite responses that have been memorized ahead of time, the highest rating you are likely to receive is Novice High. This indicates that your speech sample contains much language that has been memorized and recalled.

Below are indicators that raters will recognize as recited, memorized responses.

A speaker may:
- Recite responses that are in wide circulation. Raters hear the same response repeated by hundreds of test-takers. This signals the rater that you are reciting responses that are not your own, and therefore may not be able to engage in actual interpersonal conversations. Recent examples include stories about the following:
  - Twisted ankle
  - Spilled coffee on white pants
  - Changing wallpaper that had mold on it, the project takes a half a day
  - Interest in music, you usually like ballads, but sometimes you like to listen to upbeat music when working out or driving
  - Coming upon a concert on the beach with Psy and others who all did their signature numbers
  - Running into someone while on the phone, who later becomes your boyfriend/girlfriend/spouse
  - Living in a house with a garden as a child, but now you have to be considerate of your neighbors because you live in an apartment
  - Getting locked in the bathroom, at home or on vacation
  - Having the computer freeze while working on an important paper that is due in one hour
  - Spending time at home on your last vacation, first with family, then meeting old friends from school, one of them is getting married; you also did some soul searching and thought about your career and future
  - Placing an online order that didn't arrive
  - Recycling as a community event; getting candy as a child from the person collecting recycling
  - Borrowing a friend's wireless mouse that broke
- Repeat the exact same answer or substantial parts of it in response to more than one prompt.
- Provide a response that is not related to the question.
- Provide a response that is related to a different OPIc prompt that may or may not even occur in that particular test.
- Perform a Role Play situation that was not asked for, or pretend to be in a Role Play situation when the question does not call for it.

**Reminder to OPIc Test-Takers**

You want to show your spoken language ability at its best. In order to do so, express your own meaning using spontaneous language when responding to OPIc prompts. Address the topic and question that is asked. Remember that reciting scripted responses will result in a Novice-level rating.